Contents

Acknowledgements

We are grateful to the following for permission to reproduce copyright material:

Macmillan Accounts and Administration Ltd/University of Pittsburgh Press for an extract from *Discovering Suicide: Studies in the Social Organisation of Sudden Death* by J. Maxwell Atkinson, © 1978 by J. Maxwell Atkinson; Macmillan Accounts and Administration Ltd/St. Martin's Press Inc. for an extract from *Durkheim and the Study of Suicide* by S. Taylor; Penguin Books Ltd for an extract from *Suicide and Attempted Suicide* by Erwin Stengel, copyright © the Estate of Erwin Stengel 1964, 1970.

SOCIOLOGY IN FOCUS SERIES
General Editor: Murray Morison

The Sociology of Suicide

Steve Taylor B.A., LL.B., M.Phil., Ph.D.
Lecturer in Medical Sociology
King's College and the
London School of Economics,
University of London

LONGMAN
London and New

LONGMAN GROUP UK LIMITED

Longman House, Burnt Mill, Harlow, Essex CM20 2JE, UK
and Associated Companies throughout the World.

**Published in the United States of America
by Longman Inc., New York.**

First published 1988
ISBN 0 582 35565 6

Set in 10/11pt Bembo, Linotron 202

Produced by Longman Group (FE) Ltd
Printed in Hong Kong

British Library Cataloguing in Publication Data
Taylor, Steve, *1948–*
   The sociology of suicide.
   1. Suicide
   I. Title
   362.2

   ISBN 0-582-35565-6

Library of Congress Cataloging-in-Publication Data
Taylor, Steve (Steve D.)
   The sociology of suicide.

   (Sociology in focus series)
   Bibliography: p.
   Includes index.
   1. Suicide. I. Title. II. Series.
HV6545.T367 1988   362.2   88-535
ISBN 0-582-35565-6

Series introduction

Sociology in Focus aims to provide an up-to-date, coherent coverage of the main topics that arise on an introductory course in sociology. While the intention is to do justice to the intricacy and complexity of current issues in sociology, the style of writing has deliberately been kept simple. This is to ensure that the student coming to these ideas for the first time need not become lost in what can appear initially as jargon.

Each book in the series is designed to show something of the purpose of sociology and the craft of the sociologist. Throughout the different topic areas the interplay of theory, methodology and social policy have been highlighted, so that rather than sociology appearing as an unwieldy collection of facts, the student will be able to grasp something of the process whereby sociological understanding is developed. The format of the books is broadly the same throughout. Part 1 provides an overview of the topic as a whole. In Part 2 the relevant research is set in the context of the theoretical, methodological and policy issues. The student is encouraged to make his or her own assessment of the various arguments, drawing on the statistical and reference material provided both here and at the end of the book. The final part of the book contains both statistical material and a number of 'Readings'. Questions have been provided in this section to direct students to analyse the materials presented in terms of both theoretical assumptions and methodological approaches. It is intended that this format should enable students to exercise their own sociological imaginations rather than to see sociology as a collection of universally accepted facts, which just have to be learned.

While each book in the series is complete within itself, the similarity of format ensures that the series as a whole provides an integrated and balanced introduction to sociology. It is intended that the text can be used both for individual and classroom study while the inclusion of the varied statistical and documentary materials lend themselves to both the preparation of essays and brief seminars.

PART 1

Introduction and overview

1 What is the sociology of suicide?

At first sight suicide may appear to be a topic quite unsuited to sociological analysis. Most people tend to think of suicide as an essentially *individual* tragedy, the result of something that has 'gone wrong' with the life of the person who commits the act. For example, he or she is mentally ill, addicted to alcohol or drugs, unable to cope with the loss of a loved one, or simply too old or feeble to carry on. What have such actions got to do with *collective* social life, which is the subject matter of sociology? In answer to this question, sociologists have tried to show that even such a seemingly 'anti-social' act as suicide – which is normally undertaken by one individual in isolation from others – is still subject to certain patterns and regularities which may be induced by the nature of the social group of which the individual was a member. In attempting to explain suicide in this way, sociologists are also interested in making certain *general statements* about the relationship between individual action and group life.

This book is about the sociology of suicide. It examines the various ways in which sociologists have studied suicide, discusses some of the main criticisms of their work and considers what conclusions we can draw from their research. In Chapter 3 we shall look at the theory and method of the traditional sociological approach to suicide, paying particular attention to the pioneering work of the French sociologist **Emile Durkheim** (*Suicide*, 1897, translated in 1952). In Chapter 4 we examine criticisms of this approach, especially the debate concerning the use of official suicide statistics. Chapters 5 and 6 consider some alternative sociological approaches to suicide. This analysis is supplemented and illustrated in Part 3 by extracts from some of the most important texts in this area. Finally, the main points will be summarised and specifically related to some of the most important questions raised by the sociology of suicide.

After a careful reading of the text students should be able to understand and explain:

1 why suicide is such an important topic for sociology;
2 the *core* elements of Durkheim's theory of suicide and the *distinctive* features of the traditional sociological approach to suicide;
3 the main *methodological* problems of the sociology of suicide, especially problems associated with the use of official suicide statistics;
4 the distinction between the traditional sociological approach to suicide and alternative sociological studies based on an *interpretive* approach;
5 how certain *specific* debates and problems within the sociology of suicide reflect more *general* issues in sociology.

The first task, however, is to provide an introduction to the main issues covered in the sociology of suicide.

2 Themes in the sociology of suicide

The purpose of this chapter is merely to *introduce* you to the main questions raised by the sociology of suicide. In Part 2 we shall attempt to answer them.

1 What is the main sociological approach to suicide?

Most sociologists who have studied suicide have made a distinction between the explanation of *individual* cases of suicide and the explanation of a society's *suicide rate* – that is, the number of people in that society who kill themselves in a given period of time.

The examination of suicide rates has purported to show that there are variations in the suicide rates of different societies and of different social groups within a society, and that these rates remain remarkably consistent over time. This is illustrated by the following table adapted from Durkheim's study of suicide.

Table 1.1   Rates of suicide per million inhabitants in different European countries

	1866–70	*1871–75*	*1875–78*
Italy	30	35	38
England	67	66	69
France	135	150	160
Saxony	293	267	334

Source: E. Durkheim, *Suicide*, Routledge & Kegan Paul, 1952

Why are these variations in suicide rates so stable? Why, for example, does France not have a higher suicide rate than England in one period and a lower suicide rate in another? Sociologists have argued that the consistency of the suicide rates can only be explained in terms of these societies' differing forms of social life and social organisation. In other words, sociologists attempt to show that the social characteristics of population A explain why it has a suicide rate that is consistently higher than population B.

For a long time in the study of suicidal behaviour there developed something of a division of labour between academic disciplines. Psychiatrists and psychologists tended to study and explain why particular individuals killed themselves, while sociologists looked for the social causes of a society's, or social group's, suicide rate. However, as we shall see later, not all sociologists study suicide in this way. Therefore, for purposes of clarity, we shall refer to the sociological study of suicide rates as the 'traditional sociological approach' to suicide.

The study of suicide is a particularly important subject of enquiry for sociology. The traditional sociological approach does not only look for the social causes of suicide; it has wider aims. Sociologists, as we shall discover, use the study of suicide rates to make certain *general sociological statements*. First, they argue that the comparative study of suicide rates (that is, why population A has a higher suicide rate than population B) can tell us a great deal about the nature of different types of society. Secondly, sociologists claim that the consistency of the suicide rates and their apparent relation to social influences demonstrates conclusively the extent to which even such an 'individual' act as suicide has its roots in society. This, in turn, acts as powerful *evidence* in favour of the importance of a sociological approach to human behaviour.

Sociological studies of suicide rates, and Durkheim's in particular, had a major influence on both the development and general acceptance of sociology as an distinct academic subject. However, sociological studies of suicide, despite being grounded in the apparently 'hard' and objective data of official statistics, have also been subject to much critical comment.

2 What are the main criticisms of the traditional sociological approach to suicide?

There are two main lines of criticism of the traditional sociological approach. First, there are those who question the *reliability* of the official suicide rates on which most sociological studies are based.

These critics argue that the *meaning* of suicide does not arise automatically from a particular act, but is a product of *social definition*. That is, certain officials, called coroners and coroners' officers, have to *decide* whether or not a particular death is due to suicide or some other cause. In practice, in most cases that are referred to them, coroners have to decide whether the death is a suicide or an accident. If the officials cannot decide one way or another, then an 'open' verdict will be brought in. Open verdicts are not part of the suicide statistics.

Officials in different countries, or even in different parts of the same country, may go about this difficult task in very different ways. If this is the case, then it will clearly influence the nature of the statistics themselves. Let us illustrate this important point with an imaginary example. Suppose we are studying two towns, A-town and B-town. Both have populations of 100,000. However, while the suicide rate of A-town is 20 per year, that of B-town is only 10 per year.

How are we to try and explain this? One method would be to follow the traditional sociological approach and see if we could identify features of the social life of the two towns which might help to explain the differences in their suicide rates. However, another method would be to explore how the coroners of the two towns go about deciding whether or not a person has killed himself. We might find, for example, that whereas the coroner of A-town decided each case on a balance of probabilities, the coroner of B-town wanted much more conclusive proof, such as a suicide note, or a statement from a witness that the deceased person had actually said he or she was going to commit suicide, before considering registering the death as a suicide.

If we did find that the coroners of the two towns were employing very different criteria in order to decide whether or not a particular death was a suicide, then we would be justified in questioning the value of research based on comparing the two sets of statistics. The differences that we observed above between the suicide rates of the two towns may simply be due to differing *collection procedures*.

From this point of view sociologists of suicide from Durkheim onwards have been taken to task for their *uncritical acceptance* of the official suicide rates. Critics of the traditional sociological approach argue that one of the first tasks of the sociology of suicide should be to examine how it is that certain deaths come to be defined as 'suicides'. This question reflects – and provides a useful illustration of – a more general debate in the social sciences between those who approach the study of society with the topic of study already defined as crime or suicide or whatever, and those who adopt a more *sceptical* approach and argue that sociology has first to explain how members of society come to *label* certain things as 'suicides' or 'crimes' and so on.

In Chapter 4 we shall examine this debate in relation to suicide and suicide statistics. We shall consider the arguments against the uses of official suicide statistics, the research findings on which they are based and the implications for the traditional sociological approach to suicide.

The second major criticism of the traditional sociological approach argues that, by confining themselves to the statistics (irrespective of their reliability), sociologists have misunderstood the nature of suicidal behaviour. They have tended to accept the 'common-sense' view of suicide, that it is a self-inflicted death undertaken by someone who has formed a clear intention to die. In fact, it is not nearly as simple as this. Detailed research into the situations in which people harm themselves, the ways they go about doing it and so on, shows that most serious acts of self-harm, including many of those that actually end in death, involve *risk taking*. That is, the individual is not wholeheartedly seeking death, but rather is *gambling* with life and death in some strange form of 'game'.

Similarly, research has shown that many people *communicate* their suicidal intentions to others before a suicidal act. The risk taking and communicative aspects of suicide have important implications for the ways in which we attempt to understand and explain suicidal behaviour. For example, why do some people risk their lives in a suicidal act, whereas others go about it in a more or less efficient way? Why do some people communicate their intentions while others do not? Such questions are outside the scope of the traditional sociological approach, which does not look at suicidal behaviour as such, but only at suicide statistics. Critics argue that, for this reason, traditional sociological studies of suicide tend to be very limited in scope and are, therefore, unlikely to provide a full explanation of suicide.

3   What are the alternative sociological approaches to suicide?

For a long time the main alternative approach to suicide came from sociologists committed to an *interpretive* approach. This view holds that sociological explanation begins by trying to make sense of the meanings that *individuals* give to their own actions, or conduct. As far as possible, these meanings should be studied in the social situations in which they arise. From this point of view the traditional sociological approach is criticised for giving insufficient consideration to the individual's intentions, the *purpose* that he or she sees in his or her own actions.

The American sociologist **Jack Douglas** (*The Social Meanings of Suicide*, 1967) is one of the main proponents of an interpretive approach to the study of suicide. Having criticised Durkheim's approach, Douglas goes on to argue that sociologists should be using sources of data that bring them as close as possible to the inner world of the suicidal person; this would include data such as suicide notes, autobiographical accounts by suicidal people, diaries, case histories and interviews with attempted suicides. The object is to collect a variety of intimate or, in Douglas's terms, 'real-world' suicidal experiences. He argues that it is only when we have done this that we shall be in a position to classify, or group, types of suicidal behaviour and relate them to particular social settings or social groups.

As we shall see, while the interpretive approach to suicide advanced by Douglas and others offers an alternative to the traditional sociological view, it does not *in itself* necessarily solve the problems that have been identified in relation to the traditional view. For example, most sociologists (whatever approach they have adopted) have still worked with the idea that suicide implies some clear-cut intention on the part of the social actor to die.

More recently, however, sociologists have begun to build the key ideas of risk taking and communication into theories of suicide. In an earlier book – *Durkheim and the Study of Suicide* (1982) – I have argued that an interpretive view of suicide can in fact be combined with some of Durkheim's most important insights in order to give a more complete theoretical perspective on a range of suicidal behaviours. In Part 3 we shall examine these issues in more detail by examining original research, and statistical and documentary sources. In the concluding chapter we shall draw the various arguments together, make some general statements about the sociology of suicide and consider how we might approach some of the issues most frequently raised in relation to this topic.

PART 2

Sociological explanations of suicide

---

3 The traditional sociological approach to suicide

The aim of Durkheim's *Suicide*

Although written nearly a century ago, **Durkheim's** *Suicide* (1897, translated in 1952) remains one of the most important works in sociology. This book has done more than any other single study to establish sociology as an independent academic subject with its own distinct field of enquiry. The famous American sociologist Robert Merton (*On Theoretical Sociology*, 1967) has described it as perhaps the greatest piece of sociological research ever done.

─At the time Durkheim was writing, some people studying society thought that human behaviour was the result of the individual's free will, or choice, while others thought that it was determined or caused by racial or some form of inherited psychological characteristics. Both approaches, however, assumed that societies were merely the products of individual actions and that the study of the *individual* was therefore the key to understanding society. Even those early social scientists who did go beyond the individual tended to see human actions as caused by geographical or climatic influences.

Durkheim's distinct contribution to social science in general, and to sociology in particular, was to show the extent to which individual actions, rather than being caused by 'natural' forces within the individual or the physical environment, were shaped by the *organisation of social life*. His position was as follows. Sociology is the study of society. Society is, of course, made up of individuals. But it is something *more* than the mere sum of those individuals. In Durkheim's terms, society is not *reducible* to individuals. People are born into societies which are already organised. Societies have their own rules, values and norms, and these shape and influence people's behaviour in ways that they themselves may not realise.

Although Durkheim was not opposed to psychology – the science of the individual – his point was, rather, that the individual could not be fully understood in isolation from the society of which he or she was a member. According to Durkheim, the task of sociology should be to fill this gap by illustrating and explaining the *relationship* between social, or collective, life and individual behaviour.

Durkheim had already argued this principle in an earlier book called *The Rules of Sociological Method* (1895, translated in 1950). But many of his fellow students of society remained unconvinced. They argued that while Durkheim had *claimed* that individual action was determined by society (rather than the other way round), he had not *demonstrated* that this was so. In effect, they asked Durkheim to *prove* his case, and this was the task that he set for himself in *Suicide*. Durkheim chose the subject of suicide for such a demonstration because he felt that if he could show that even such a supremely 'individual' act as suicide was influenced by society, then he would have proved his case by the very act seemingly most unfavourable to it.

Durkheim's explanation of suicide

By the middle of the nineteenth century most European countries were compiling suicide statistics. It soon became clear, as we observed in Part 1, that not only were there significant variations in the suicide rates of different populations, but also that these variations remained remarkably consistent over time.

Why were the suicide rates so consistent? Durkheim dismissed earlier explanations based on climate, race, rates of mental illness and imitation. For Durkheim, the stability of the suicide rates was a social fact and must, therefore, be explained sociologically. He attempted to show that the differences in suicide rates were the results of different forms of social life. In Durkheim's terms, social groups had their own 'collective inclination' to suicide, and it was this that he sought to explain in his book.

However, before we can understand Durkheim's theory of suicide it is necessary to know something about his conception of social and moral order. The *problem of social order* – the question of how societies came into being and hold together – is one of the most fundamental issues in sociology. Indeed, almost all sociological works in one way or another are addressed to this question. Durkheim's explanation of this problem was that social order is possible because individual's basic drives are limited, or constrained, by the forces generated by collective social life. According to Durkheim, society constrains individuals in two ways. First, it *integrates* them by binding them to the values and norms of social groups. Secondly, it *regulates* their potentially limitless desires and aspirations by defining specific goals and means of attaining them.

Durkheim argued that without the integration and regulation of the individual by society human life would be chaos and, indeed, he suggested that certain 'pathological', or deviant, trends in modern society (such as the steady increase in suicide rates) were to be explained in terms of the lack of integration and regulation of the individual by society. Durkheim developed four types of suicide from his conception of social and moral order (see Figure 3.1). *Egoistic* and *altruistic* suicide arose from the under- and over-integration of the individual; while *anomic* and *fatalistic* suicide stemmed from under- and over-regulation.

Figure 3.1   Durkheim's conception of social order and types of suicide

Social order	Normal form	Pathological form	Types of suicide
integration ——	when in 'balance' the individual is 'protected' from suicide	→lack of integration ——→ over-integration	——→ egoistic ——→ altruistic
regulation ——		→lack of regulation ——→ over-regulation	——→ anomic ——→ fatalistic

Egoistic suicide

Egoistic suicide results from the weakening, or diluting, of the ties binding the individual to social groups. When people become detached from the values and expectations of those around them, then they are in danger of suffering from an 'excess of individualism' and are more vulnerable to suicide.

Durkheim illustrated the existence of egoistic suicide with examples from religious, domestic and political society. The statistics showed that Catholic countries had consistently lower suicide rates than Protestant ones and, even within the same country, Catholic areas had proportionally lower suicide rates. This difference was not to be explained in terms of the different attitudes of the two religions to suicide, as both condemned it without reservation. The cause was to be found in the fact that Catholic society binds the believer into an established set of traditional beliefs and practices common to all the faithful. In contrast, Protestantism, which allows a greater spirit of free enquiry and has far less in the way of common beliefs and practices, provided a less integrated community than Catholicism. Protestants, therefore, tended to be more prone to egoism than Catholics. In times of crisis the Protestant was more likely to be thrown back on to his or her own resources and was thus more vulnerable to suicide. The greater 'protection' from suicide for Catholics came not from their beliefs as such but from the more intense and integrating quality of their social life.

Secondly, the suicide rates showed that married people with children are more protected from suicide than unmarried people or childless couples. The protection comes not from marriage itself, but from the integrating effects of family life and children.

Thirdly, Durkheim also observed that suicide rates tended to decline in times of war or political upheaval. This is because increasing numbers of individuals identify themselves with a 'common cause'. They are thus more integrated into collective life and, at least temporarily, less vulnerable to suicide.

There are, then, statistical associations, or correlations, between suicide rates and types of religion, family life and political activity. However, it is important to grasp that Durkheim was *not* suggesting that these factors are *in themselves* cause of differences in the suicide rates. Rather, he was using the relationship between suicide and religious, family and political life to reveal *a common, underlying cause of suicide*, which was the extent to which individuals are integrated into the social groups around them. In modern Western society, the more individuals are integrated into society the more protected they are from suicide. Thus Durkheim advanced the following proposition: 'Suicide varies inversely with the degree of integration of the social groups of which the individual forms a part.'

Altruistic suicide

Altruistic suicide is the opposite of egoistic suicide. It is caused by the over-integration of the individual into the social group. In altruistic suicide the individual's ego, rather than being too great, is too weak to resist the demands of society that he or she must commit suicide. In such cases the individual's identity has become dissolved into the social group. The ritualistic suicide of a woman on the death of her husband or that of a military chief after defeat in battle or dishonour are examples of altruistic suicide. Such suicidal deaths are demanded by custom and tradition. By committing suicide, the individual is not deviating from, but rather conforming to, social norms.

Durkheim considered that altruistic suicide was largely confined to 'primitive' or 'traditional' societies. However, such suicides are not unknown in modern times. Captain Oates's celebrated 'last walk' into the snow to give his comrades on Scott's ill-fated expedition to the South Pole a better chance of survival, or the last missions of the Japanese kamikaze pilots, may properly be classified as altruistic suicides. A more recent example of altruistic suicide is found in the Jonestown massacres, where hundreds of people in an enclosed religious community in Guyana in 1978 killed themselves and their children at the command of their leader, the Reverend Jim Jones.

When the Reverend Jim Jones learned that Congressman Ryan had been killed but that some members of his [investigating] party had survived, Jones called together the followers of his People's Temple Community and told them the time had come to commit the mass suicide they had rehearsed several times. 'They started with the babies,' Odell Rhodes told me when I visited Jonestown to view the 405 bodies – men, women and children – most of them grouped round the altar where Jones himself lay dead. Rhodes is the only known survivor of the Jonestown community who witnessed part of the suicide rite before managing to escape. Most of those who drank the deadly poison did so willingly. . . . It took about five minutes for the liquid to take its final effect, young and old, black and white grouped themselves, usually near other family members often with their arms round each other, waiting for the cyanide to kill them. All the while Jones was urging them on, explaining that they would 'meet in another place'.

(*Guardian*, 22 November 1978)

Anomic suicide

Anomic suicide arises from the lack of regulation of the individual by society. The statistics showed that suicide rates rise in periods of economic depression and, perhaps more surprisingly, in times of economic prosperity. Why should this be so? According to Durkheim, the cause of this fluctuation is not simply greater poverty or prosperity, but rather the social and individual *instability* brought about by such changes.

In times of rapid economic fluctuation increasing numbers of individuals find themselves in changed social circumstances. Whether people find themselves in positions of increased poverty or prosperity, the norms and social values which had previously regulated their conduct are placed under increasing strain as they become less relevant to their new and changing situations. When this happens, the individual is placed in a situation of moral deregulation, or anomie, and is thus more vulnerable to suicide.

The specific changes in the suicide rate that accompany periods of economic depression and prosperity are merely acute examples of what Durkheim felt was a general and pathological condition of modern society. Modern western society tends to promote competition and self-interest. It encourages increasing numbers of individuals to want more than they have at any given time. As people are always wanting more than they have, it follows that they can never be satisfied. The continuing and unbridgeable gap between what people actually have and what they desire to have produces a source of dissatisfaction and frustration which makes suicide more likely.

You will read in some books that Durkheim was essentially a conservative thinker, opposed to change and critical of social dissent – in short, a defender of the status quo. Little could be further from the truth. Durkheim felt that the acquisitive, self-interested norms and values of modern western society,

Jackie

encouraging as they did continuing dissatisfaction and discontent, had done little to improve human happiness. On the contrary, they generated more anomic states which, above all, were responsible for the pathological, steady rise in suicide rates. Durkheim was not criticising discontent as such, but rather the norms and values which tended to produce the 'unquenchable thirst' of *never-ending* discontent. In his way Durkheim was just as profound a critic of modern western society as Marx and Weber.

Fatalistic suicide

Fatalistic suicide, the opposite of anomic suicide, results from the over-regulation of the individual. Durkheim considered that this type of suicide was of little importance in modern society and he only discussed it in a footnote. However, as we shall see in Chapter 5, some later students of suicide have attached more relevance to the concept.

Summary of Durkheim's *Suicide*

When we look at individual cases of suicide in isolation from one another, we tend to look for the causes in things, such as a state of mind or social situation, which are specific to the individual concerned. However, this does not explain why the numbers of people who kill themselves in a given social group are so consistent over time. To explain this problem we must look beyond the immediate and 'individual' causes.

Durkheim argued that the regularity of suicide rates was a social fact; that is, it can only be explained in terms of the differing forms of social life of various social groups. Durkheim held that in modern society there were two principle causes of high (and rising) suicide rates: (egoistic) suicide was higher where individuals were not well integrated into collective social life; and (anomic) suicide was higher when society's norms and values were too weak to regulate individual desires and drives.

The relationship between levels of social integration and regulation and suicide rates demonstrated that society exerted an independent influence over the individual. In Durkheim's terms, society was *external* to the individual, so much so that even such a supremely individual act as suicide had its roots in society.

Post-Durkheimian studies of suicide rates

We have already observed that Durkheim's work had a profound influence on the development of sociology as a whole. As far as the sociology of suicide was concerned, Durkheim's book appeared to have given sociology a distinct research model, or paradigm, within which to work. Most sociologists have accepted that the 'sociological task' in this field is to focus on suicide rates, and try to explain their variations in terms of social influences such as social factors or social structures.

However, in this context, it is important to bear in mind two points. First, as we shall see in Chapters 4 and 5, some sociologists have been very critical of Durkheim's approach to sociology in general and his study of suicide in particular. Secondly, even those sociologists who *appear* to be following in the 'Durkheimian tradition' have some significant reservations about Durkheim's theory, as we shall see at the end of this chapter.

Although there have been hundreds of subsequent studies of suicide rates (not all by sociologists), no one since Durkheim has attempted to construct such a complete, embracing theory of suicide. Many later studies have restricted themselves either to 'testing' the relationship between suicide and particular variables, or to refining and developing aspects of Durkheim's theory. For example, J. Marshall and R. Hodge (in *Social Science Research* 10.2, 1981) found correlations between suicide and economic disruption, while the findings of K. Breault and K. Barkey (in *The Sociological Quarterly* 23.3, 1983) were similar to those of Durkheim on the relationship between suicide and religious, political and domestic society. This section will not attempt a comprehensive review of the post-Durkheimian work, but will focus on a few of the more important later studies in order to illustrate the development and general characteristics of the traditional sociological approach to suicide.

Social integration/social isolation

One of the first major sociological studies of suicide rates to follow Durkheim's work was in fact undertaken by one of his own students, **M. Halbwachs** (*Les Causes du suicide*, 1930). Although his work confirmed most of Durkheim's findings, Halbwachs developed a rather more simple explanation of suicide.

He observed that suicide rates tended to become lower as one moved from the densely populated cities towards the more rural areas.

Halbwachs argued that many of the correlations observed by Durkheim could be explained more effectively in terms of the differing ways of life of urban and rural subcultures. For example, the reason why Catholic populations had relatively lower suicide rates than Protestant ones had less to do with religion than with the fact that the Catholic communities were located predominantly in rural areas.

Halbwachs argued that suicide was relatively higher in urban areas because the urban way of life was more transitory and impersonal, and left increasing numbers of individuals *socially isolated* from their fellows and hence more vulnerable to suicide. Many other studies have subsequently confirmed a positive link between social isolation and suicide. **P. Sainsbury** (*Suicide in London*, 1955), for example, studied the suicide rate of London boroughs, and found that those districts with the highest rates of social isolation (and social mobility) tended to be the ones that produced most suicide. Similarly, **R. Cavan** (*Suicide*, 1965), studying the suicide rates of the districts of Chicago, found that suicides were highest in those districts characterised by low social integration and high rates of social mobility and 'social disorganisation'.

Such research tends to support Durkheim's key idea of low levels of social integration producing high rates of suicide. However, two American sociologists, **J. Gibbs and W. Martin** (*Status Integration and Suicide: A Sociological Study*, 1964) have observed that even this fundamental part of Durkheim's theory could not be subject to formal, empirical testing as he provided no clear workable, or operational, definition as to exactly what he meant by 'social integration'.

Gibbs and Martin agree with Durkheim that social integration is almost certainly a very important influence on suicide. They hypothesise that the suicide rate of a population will vary inversely with the stability and durability of social relationships within that population. However, the problem is that one cannot measure stability and durability of social relationships over time. Therefore Gibbs and Martin approach their target by another, more round-about route. They develop the more limited, but more easily identifiable, concept of *status integration*.

A status is the social position that one occupies in a social group. Typically, a person occupies a number of statuses: for example, male–lawyer–married–father–Protestant. The less these statuses are integrated with each other (that is, the less 'overlap' there is in their tenancy), then the more individuals are subject to role conflict. This, in turn, impairs the stability and durability of social relationships and makes a higher suicide rate more likely. In short, Gibbs and Martin are attempting to use the more 'concrete' concept of status integration to measure the more intangible notion of social integration. From this basis they hypothesise that the suicide rate of a population varies inversely with the degree of status integration of that population. They claim that the data available on status integration tend to support their theory (although these data are in fact limited).

Gibbs and Martin argued that they have identified an important weakness in Durkheim's theory and remedied it with the development of the more testable theory of status integration. However, there are important problems with Gibbs' and Martin's own approach. First, they conceive of status integration only in *statistical* terms and do not consider the meaning that particular statuses have to individuals in given situations. For example, there are few males who are politicians, whereas there are relatively more female married social workers, yet it seems reasonable to suppose that there may well be more 'role conflict' among the latter group. Secondly, as Gibbs and Martin provide no evidence to show that the individuals who actually kill themselves suffer from a low degree of status integration, their own theory can hardly be said to have been tested.

Gibbs' and Martin's work is significant, however, in so far as it illustrates how sociologists have tried to work within and clarify the framework provided by Durkheim. It also draws attention to the importance of trying to 'test' key causal concepts rather than merely assuming that they are valid.

Status change

As we have seen, Durkheim argued that modern societies were producing conditions, such as rapid economic change, in which increasing numbers of individuals were likely to find themselves in situations of 'normlessness' or anomie. Such 'deregulation' was favourable to the growth of anomic suicide. The notion that a change of status, especially loss of status, is positively related to suicide has subsequently become one of the most firmly established in the sociology of suicide.

J. Gibbs and A. Porterfield (in *American Journal of Sociology* 66, 1960) made a study of New Zealand suicide statistics which, from the researchers' point of view, had the advantage of giving the victim's occupational class at birth and death. They found positive correlations between both 'upward' and 'downward' occupational mobility and suicide. Gibbs and Porterfield argued that this was because social mobility tends to produce relatively more anxiety (if upward) or feelings of failure and frustration (if downward), and also it weakens social ties, so that in times of personal crisis the individual tends to have less social support.

In one of the most original and interesting studies of suicide rates **A. Henry and J. Short** (*Suicide and Homicide*, 1954) found, similarly to Durkheim, that suicide rates (and homicide rates) rose in periods of economic recession. They also found that suicide was relatively more prevalent among 'high status' groups, whereas homicide was relatively more common among the 'lower status' groups.

Why should this be so? Henry and Short's explanation runs as follows. Both suicide and homicide are acts of aggression: in suicide the aggression is directed against the self, while in homicide it is directed at another or others. Periods of economic recession and hardship tend to produce more frustration in individuals, which in some cases then stimulates aggressive impulses. Higher status individuals are less *externally restrained* by others than individuals in lower statuses. That means that in social relations with others the higher the individual's status the more likely it is that he or she will play the superior rather than the subordinate role. Thus when higher status individuals feel frustration, they have fewer available targets for their aggression and, other things being equal, they are more likely to direct it at themselves. For Henry and Short it is the rising rates of suicide within the higher status populations that are largely responsible for the rise in the overall suicide rate in times of economic depression.

Social-psychological theories

As we shall see more clearly in Chapter 6, Durkheim's theory of suicide was essentially a social-psychological theory. That is, he was interested in exploring the relationship between the collective organisation of social life and the individual, or personal, experience of suicide. In contrast, most later sociological works on suicide have confined themselves to examining social influences on suicide which are *external* to the individual. We can use the term 'sociologistic', or 'social determinism', to describe such approaches. Sociologistic works on suicide, such as those by Gibbs and Martin and Henry and Short, effectively *preclude* any serious consideration of the psychological dimensions of suicide.

However, some researchers have attempted to identify some of the social-psychological influences that might help to explain the link between sociological conditions and the psychological tendency to be more likely to commit suicide. One such avenue of exploration has been the possible relationship between patterns of child rearing, socialisation and suicide.

We have already observed, when looking at the work of Henry and Short, that higher status persons tend to be relatively more prone to suicide than lower status persons. Henry and Short explained this in terms of the lack of physical external restraint from others. **M. Gold** (1958) offers an alternative, social-psychological explanation. He argues that the answer is to be found in the different child-rearing practices of middle- and working-class families. Working-class children are more likely to be punished physically, whereas middle-class children are more likely to receive more punishment of a psychological nature. Children who are punished physically, rather than psychologically, are more likely themselves to express more direct, outward physical aggression. With psychological punishment, on the other hand, it is more difficult to tell where the 'hurt' feelings come from. There is more likelihood that the psychologically punished child will blame himself or herself for bringing the punishment about in the first place. Middle-class children are thus more likely to 'learn' to direct their aggression inwards against themselves.

A broadly similar approach was taken by **H. Hendin** (1964) in his study of suicide in Scandinavia. Hendin was interested in why the suicide rate of Norway was so much lower than those of both Sweden and Denmark. He also argued that the crucial factor was the differing child-rearing techniques of each culture. Because Norwegian children are not expected to suppress emotional expression, they are 'emotionally freer' as adults than Swedes and Danes and are less likely to turn aggression inwards

against themselves. This, according to Hendin, is a crucial factor
in explaining Norway's relatively lower suicide rate.

Comparison between Durkheim's work and later sociological studies

So far, we have examined Durkheim's approach to suicide and
looked at its influence on later works by other sociologists.
However, we should also bear in mind that there are some
significant *differences* between Durkheim's study and later
sociological works.

We have already touched on some of these differences. First,
Durkheim's theory was all-embracing and attempted to account
for all suicidal acts, whereas later studies of suicide rates have
tended to be more limited in scope. Secondly, Durkheim's theory
was social-psychological, while most later studies of suicide rates
have looked only at social factors actually 'outside' the individual.
We must also consider another, rather complex, theoretical
difference. Most later studies of suicide rates are *positivist*, whereas
Durkheim's theory of suicide was not. Durkheim did want sociology to be scientific (and this distinguishes him from those who
advocate an interpretive approach), but he had a different view
of science from that held by the positivists. For the positivist
science involves observing the relationships between things (or
phenomena) and trying to identify what causes what. However,
for Durkheim, science involved searching for the invisible, underlying causes of the relationships between the things that are
observed.

The technical term for Durkheim's approach is '*realist*', whereas
positivist studies, such as those by Gibbs and Martin or Henry
and Short, adopt a *nominalist* view. The nominalist view holds
that science (and social science) should only concern itself with
'facts', which it sees as things directly available to human
experience. In contrast, realists speculate that the causes of many
of the things we observe lie in 'facts' which are outside our direct
experience. Thus, in the social sciences, whereas positivists focus
on relationships between observable parts of society and nothing
else, realists, like Durkheim, view society as something more than
the sum of its parts.

In his study of suicide Durkheim did not, therefore, limit himself to the relationship between suicide rates and social factors, such as religion, family density and so on. He went on to explain these relationships in terms of real, but invisible, social forces: currents of egoism, anomie and altruism (Table 3.1).

Table 3.1   Levels of explanation in Durkheim's Suicide

I Problem to be explained	II Observable indicators of suicide	III Explanation of suicide
The stability of, and differences between, suicide rates	Suicide related positively to, e.g. religious affiliation, family structure, social and political change, etc.	Currents of egoism, anomie and altruism

In general, later sociological students of suicide were impressed by Durkheim's demonstration of the relationships between suicide rates and a variety of social factors, but they were less enthusiastic about his attempts to explain these relationships in terms of the 'invisible forces' of egoism, anomie and altruism. For such positivists, this aspect of Durkheim's work was 'unscientific' because he was arguing for the existence of social facts (such as egoism) which could not be perceived by direct, or sensory, experience.

A long discussion of the rival merits of realist and nominalist approaches to social science lies outside the scope of this book. However, we can note that (perhaps because of the apparent 'failure' of positivism to produce a scientific sociology) much current opinion in the philosophy of science and the sociology of knowledge favours a realist view of science and social science. For this reason there has been a renewed and more enlightened interest in Durkheim's work. It is unfortunate, therefore, that some textbook writers still persist in placing Durkheim within the positivist tradition. As far as the sociology of suicide is concerned, it is important to appreciate both the similarities and the differences between Durkheim's approach to suicide rates and that taken by later sociologists. In summary of this point we can conclude that, while there is a *methodological* similarity between Durkheim's work and later studies, there are some important *theoretical* differences.

Summary

This final section draws together some of the arguments we have discussed earlier and summarises the main assumptions of the traditional sociological approach to suicide.

1 There is a distinction between the explanation of individual acts of suicide and the explanation of suicide rates: the sociologist's concern is with the latter.
2 The stability of suicide rates is a social fact, and differences between suicide rates are to be explained in terms of different types of social order.
3 Lack of social integration and changes in social status appear to be two of the main causes of high suicide rates.
4 Examination of individual cases of suicide and individual motives are largely irrelevant to the sociology of suicide.
5 Sociological work in this area is largely confined to completed suicide; that is; those suicidal acts which actually end in death.

We have seen how Durkheim's work provided a distinct research framework for the sociological analysis of suicide. Most sociologists working in this field have concentrated on *specific* problems within this research framework, as we saw, for example, with Gibbs' and Martin's attempt to construct a more 'testable' concept of social integration.

However, there are sociologists (and others) who have raised more *general* doubts about the traditional sociological approach to suicide. These criticisms can be divided into two broad areas. First, there are those who have criticised sociologists' general acceptance of official suicide statistics. Second, there are those who question sociologists' reluctance to explore the circumstances and micro-social contexts of suicidal actions, including suicidal actions that do not end in death. The next three chapters are devoted to these issues. Chapter 4 focuses on the *methodological* question of the reliability of official suicide rates, while Chapters 5 and 6 explore the *conceptual* issue of what we mean by 'suicidal' actions and the *theoretical* question as to how we might best explain them.

4 The critique of official suicide rates

The social construction of official data

As we have seen from the previous chapter, the 'traditional socio-logical approach' to suicide has seen its main task as explaining the consistent variations in the distribution of suicide in terms of different forms of social life and social organisation. Although there are some important differences between particular socio-logical theories of suicide, from a *methodological* standpoint, the 'traditional sociological approach' to suicide from Durkheim onwards has been based on *the study of official suicide rates*. From the sociologist's point of view this approach has a number of advantages:

1 the data are readily available and do not have to be collected by the researcher;
2 the data provide relatively large numbers;
3 because the suicide rate is a percentage of a whole population, this enables the researcher to engage in comparative analysis of those populations;
4 when theories are 'tested' by the official suicide rates, they appear to have the additional authority of statistical 'proof'.

Of course, it is not only sociological students of suicide who make use of such sources of data. A great deal of work in sociology and social policy involves the interpretation and explanation of various types of official data. But how reliable is this source of data? Just because something is both 'official' and presented in 'statistical' form does not mean that we should necessarily take its authority for granted. It should be remembered that when we look at *particular* problems associated with official suicide rates we are, by implication, also looking at *general* issues concerned with the interpretation and use of data. Official statistics on deviant behav-iour or anything else do not simply emerge naturally. They are *socially constructed*; that is, they are produced by the negotiations and decisions of officials within various state bureaucracies.

Some sociologists have become increasingly interested in exploring the social processes whereby state bureaucratic organisations generate official data. In the case of deviant behaviour they suggest that one of the first tasks for the sociologist should be to try to understand and explain the social processes involved when labels such as 'crime', 'suicide', 'mental illness' and so on are applied to certain individuals and actions. They argue that the *meanings* of such labels cannot be taken for granted. Sociologists have first to understand how the members of various professional groups and officials apply these labels in concrete situations. Once they have done this they will be in a better position to assess the nature and quality of the 'data' produced by such decision making. In short, what these sociologists are proposing is a shift of emphasis in research away from exclusive concern with deviant behaviour and its causes towards the social processes involved in some actions being *defined* as deviant by others. They argue that the 'societal reaction' to deviance cannot be taken for granted but is itself a problem to be explained.

When we apply these arguments to the study of suicide, the implication is that we cannot take the suicide rates for granted, but rather we must question their meaning and hence their reliability for research purposes. Of course, even researchers who use the official suicide rates accept that there will be 'errors' in the reporting of suicides. In particular, it is generally accepted that some suicidal deaths will not be reported as such. For example, a person may successfully 'disguise' a suicide, relatives may lie and conceal things to try to avoid the stigma of a suicidal death in the family, or officials may simply feel that they do not have enough evidence to come to a definite conclusion one way or the other.

If this is the case, then the official statistics, at the very least, will under-estimate the volume of suicide in a given population. However, researchers who use the official figures have assumed, or have sometimes attempted to argue, that the errors in the reporting of suicide are *random* and, therefore, tend to cancel one another out. If this is so, then the statistics are still useful for research purposes, as recorded suicides would still be a *representative* sample of the total level of suicide. In contrast to this point of view other researchers – Douglas, for example – have argued that the nature of recording suicide is such that the official statistics are *systematically* biased, thus making them unacceptable for research.

Whether a set of statistics is randomly or systematically biased is a crucial point which we can illustrate with a simple example. Imagine you are looking at the results of 'learning tests' given to groups of children in different schools in order to 'monitor' the average performance levels of those schools. In school A you find that 25 per cent of the children who should have taken the test were not in school that day due to an outbreak of flu. The test results may still be taken as valid as, unless you are given evidence to the contrary, you can assume that the children who missed the test did so through chance. The non-attendance was, therefore, determined randomly, and those who took the paper can be considered a representative sample of the whole group. In school B 25 per cent of the children also did not take the tests. However, in this case you find that teachers had not given the test paper to many of the children considered to be 'less able' academically. In this case non-attendance at the test was not random, but selective. Test results would thus be systematically biased, and the sample of those who took the test would not be representative of the whole.

One of the questions that we shall try to answer in this chapter is whether the official suicide rates are more likely to be randomly or systematically biased. In practice, researchers vary in the amount of confidence that they place in the official data. For example, there are those (such as Durkheim and Gibbs and Martin) who felt enough confidence in the statistics to compare the suicide rates of different countries over relatively long periods of time, while others (Sainsbury and Cavan, for example) limited their research to the suicide rate of one particular city. However, for purposes of this discussion, we can identify two broad and opposing positions. On the one hand, there are sociologists who, despite some reservations, argue that official suicide rates (at least in 'developed' countries in recent years) are adequate for research purposes. On the other hand, there are those who argue that the problems in the collection of official suicide rates are sufficient to make them an unacceptable source of data. We may refer to the first of these positions as one of *acceptance* of official suicide rates, and the second as one of *scepticism* concerning the research value of official suicide rates.

The main differences between these positions are summarised in Table 4.1.

Table 4.1   *Sociological positions on official suicide rates*

Position	Basic assumption	Interpretation of official suicide rates	Focus of research
Acceptance	Suicide can be clearly defined and usually recognised as such by officials; the suicide rate is, therefore, a useful source of data.	Errors in the reporting of suicide tend to cancel one another out, and official suicide rates, therefore, are a representative sample of 'real' suicide rates.	Sociologists study official suicide rates and explain them in terms of social factors and other social influences.
Scepticism	Official suicide rates are socially constructed: the definitions and collection procedures of officials will vary and suicide rates will, therefore, tend to be systematically biased.	Official suicide rates are an unrepresentative sample of suicidal actions.	To examine how deaths come to be defined as 'suicides' and/or use alternative sources of data to try to explain suicide.

Douglas's work on suicide (1967) provides a good example of the *sceptical* position. He argues that there are a number of sources of systematic bias in the official suicide rates. For example, the more 'socially integrated' a community is, then, other things being equal, the more likely it is that a higher proportion of suicides will be concealed. First, relatives and friends will make a greater attempt to hide evidence of suicide. Secondly, because an individual died in an 'integrated' social situation, the less likely it is that the officials will *believe* the death could be due to suicide. What Douglas is arguing here, then, is that social integration may not necessarily be a factor in the *causation* of suicide so much as a factor influencing its *recognition* and *recording*. Douglas offers an *alternative explanation* for the finding of so many sociological studies of suicide that official suicide rates are positively related to low levels of social integration. In doing this he is casting doubt on studies based on official suicide rates.

In response to Douglas's critique, those who adopt a position of *acceptance* of official suicide rates have advanced the following defences. J. Gibbs and W. Martin (in *Social Forces* 52, 1974) raise three points: first, the researchers who use them are not claiming that the statistics are absolutely reliable but that they are *relatively* reliable; secondly, critics have not *demonstrated* the unreliability of official suicide rates; thirdly, because they need relatively large numbers to 'test' a theory, sociologists have no alternative but to use the official suicide rates. P. Cresswell (in *Journal of Biosocial Science* 6, 1974) goes further. He argues that the very stability and consistency of the official suicide rates can themselves be taken as evidence of the influence of 'social factors' on suicide.

Which of these positions – *acceptance* or *scepticism* – is more tenable? In order to begin to answer this question we must move from the level of argument and debate and begin to look at relevant research into the social construction of official suicide rates. What are the social processes involved in some deaths becoming recorded as suicides? To do this we have to turn to the work of the officials charged with this task, the coroners and their officers. We shall look first at the official functions of the coroner and secondly, at some of the interpretive procedures of the officials.

The role of the coroner's office

Most people die from illnesses. This is called 'death from natural causes'. In many such cases death is anticipated and the deceased's doctor signs a certificate indicating the cause of death. The death can then be registered and relatives allowed to proceed with arrangements for the disposal of the body. However, when a person dies suddenly and unexpectedly the case is normally referred to a coroner. It is the coroner's job to investigate how the person died. The coroner has a number of experts to assist him in this task. He may order a detailed examination of the corpse, which is called a '*post mortem*'. At the same time specially trained detectives, called coroner's officers, may carry out investigation of the circumstances surrounding the death.

In most cases the coroner's inquiry will show that death was due to natural causes and the registration of the death will then proceed in the normal manner. However, if death is not due to natural causes, the coroner's officers always investigate the possibility that the deceased was murdered. Once homicide has been ruled out, then, although in principle there are a range of complex technical verdicts open to the coroner, in practice in the majority of cases he or she has to decide whether death was due to suicide or accident. If, at the end of the inquiry, the coroner is still undecided, or if the evidence is insufficient to come to a definite conclusion, an open verdict will be returned. The main categories open to the coroner are summarised in Figure 4.1.

Most deaths which are not due to natural causes are classified as either accidents or suicides. But how does a coroner decide whether or not a person committed suicide? To take this issue further we have to move beyond the *formal* rules and concepts for categorising deaths and examine some of the *informal* rules and procedures that officials apply in day-to-day practice.

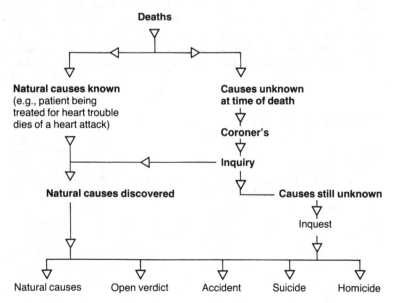

Figure 4.1 Verdicts available to a coroner

Establishing suicidal intent

For a death to be recorded as a suicide it has to be established that the deceased died as a result of his or her own actions and that he or she *intended* to die from them. This concept of suicide defines the object of the inquiry. But how is suicidal intent to be established? After all, it is quite obvious that a suicide cannot 'confess' or be 'tricked' into an admission by cross-examination in court. Therefore, suicidal intent has to be implied retrospectively; that is, by an interpretation of past events.

The coroners and their officers who undertake this task do not see their work as problematic. For them, the process is quite straightforward. There are well-established procedures for collecting evidence (including medical evidence); witnesses testify on oath in court; and, providing there is 'enough' evidence, the coroner (or jury) reach the 'correct' decision. According to this official view the decision is dictated by the evidence, or facts. However, most sociologists would question this account. It is not that this official view is wrong, but rather that it leaves a number of important questions unanswered. Pieces of 'relevant evidence', or 'significant facts' do not emerge by themselves. They have to be *selected* and *interpreted* by the observer. This selection process is structured, first by the conceptual categories available to the observer (that is, *what* he or she is looking for), and secondly, by the assumptions, ideas and beliefs that the observer takes for granted (namely, *how* he or she makes sense of the data).

In relation to the present discussion of the work of coroners, this means that we have to go 'behind' the official view and ask a number of additional questions: for example, what is relevant evidence? what influences the selection of this relevant evidence? and what does this tell us about the nature of the suicide statistics?

In his work on coroners (*Discovering Suicide*, 1978) **J. Atkinson** has shown that there are certain pieces of evidence that are taken by coroners and coroner's officers as indicators of suicidal intent. He calls these *suicidal cues* because they tend either to suggest or, later in the inquiry, to confirm, that a death was a suicide. Broadly, these suicidal cues can be divided into two areas: those which come from the scene of death (primary cues) and those that are discovered in the life history of the deceased (secondary cues).

As we shall see later in the chapter, this is an important distinction. We shall consider each type of cue in turn.

Circumstances of death (primary cues)

1   MANNER OF DEATH

Our concern here is with explaining how officials are led towards bringing in a verdict of suicide. To the lay person this might seem quite obvious. After all, there are some fairly well-established ways in which people in western society go about trying to put an end to their lives: drowning, shooting, poisoning and hanging, for example. Therefore, does not the manner of death tell us whether or not a person committed suicide? The answer to this is that, while the manner of death (and certain other evidence found at the scene of death) can provide very important suicidal cues, it does not mean that a person *necessarily* committed suicide. Even with some of the most 'well-established' means of committing suicide, there are always alternative explanations. For example, a case of drowning, or a fall from a high place or under a train nearly always raises the question (assuming murder has been ruled out) of whether the person jumped (deliberately) or fell (accidently).

Similarly, there are various possible reasons, such as ignorance, anxiety or frailty, why someone could take an overdose of tablets by mistake. Alternatively, a person could knowingly take a dangerous quantity of drugs without suicidal intent but do so, for example, for 'kicks' or, as the following case illustrates, as a 'cry for help'.

> *Tragedy of schoolgirl's guilty secret.* Sex case girl M. H. was in torment. She was being quizzed by the police about her relationship with a 30 year old man. Finally she took an overdose of drugs and died. But the move may only have been meant as a cry for help, a coroner said yesterday. Recording an open verdict [the coroner] said, 'I find it difficult to believe that she really thought at the time that she was likely to be dead in a matter of hours.'
> (S. Taylor, *Durkheim and the Study of Suicide*, Macmillan, 1982)

Even cases where the overdose is massive – say, twenty times the prescribed level – need not necessarily be suicide. Researchers in the field have discovered that even a relatively small amount of some drugs can produce something called 'automatism' – that is, a state of mind where a person continues swallowing tablets automatically quite unaware of what he or she is doing.

Once murder has been excluded, hanging is perhaps one of the most clear-cut suicidal cues. Even here, however, the possibility of accident cannot be ruled out. Some people can hang themselves accidently while practising a masochistic sexual activity involving a rope tied tightly round the neck. Others, it has been decided in court, have hanged themselves accidently while apparently trying to frighten others or re-enact some incident, as in the following case.

> *Boy's death link with record.* A suggestion that the record 'Gallows Pole' might have induced D. P., aged 16, to hang himself accidently was advanced at an inquest yesterday. A verdict of death by misadventure was recorded after the coroner said that there was no evidence that the boy intended to harm himself. . . . Detective Inspector J. A. . . . suggested that the boy put a rope round his neck in the cupboard and slipped.
> (Taylor, 1982)

2 SUICIDE NOTE

As the manner of death does not normally provide *enough* evidence to establish suicidal intent, then it might be thought that the suicide note would provide the conclusive evidence. A suicide note can be seen as the nearest equivalent to a written confession in a criminal case. In fiction, characters who kill themselves often write long and elaborate notes. The reality is somewhat different. First, notes are only recovered in a small minority of cases where suicide is suspected and, even in cases where a suicide verdict is eventually recorded, notes are only discovered in about 25 per cent of cases. Secondly, even when a note is recovered, it is not always a clear expression of suicidal motivation. In one piece of research **E. Shneidman and N. Farberow** (*Clues to Suicide*, 1957) compared a sample of deliberately faked 'suicide' notes, written by students, with a sample of apparently 'genuine' notes discovered in the course of coroners' inquiries. Interestly, it was the faked notes that tended to contain the clearest and most unambiguous statements of suicidal intent. In contrast, many of the genuine notes were shorter and more ambiguous in their meaning, often containing brief and cryptic statements such as 'I can't go on', 'Do not disturb' and 'Are you satisfied?'.

Clearly, even notes such as these, taken in conjunction with other suicidal cues from the scene of death, such as a gun-shot wound or an empty bottle of pills, can provide another important indicator of suicidal intent. However, even in the minority of cases where they are discovered, suicide notes do not necessarily provide conclusive evidence of suicidal intent.

The biography of the deceased (secondary cues)

The arguments and examples that we considered in the previous section have shown us that certain types of evidence from the circumstances of death – most importantly, the manner of death and any note written by the deceased just prior to death – provide important indicators, or cues, of suicidal intent. However, while evidence from the circumstances of death can point officials in the direction of suicide, *it is rarely, if ever, sufficient to prove suicidal intent*. It must be remembered that suicide is a *legal* concept that must be proved in a court of law beyond reasonable doubt. Therefore, in order to bring in a verdict of suicide, a coroner requires *additional evidence*. He or she requires evidence from the biography of the deceased that will justify and explain a verdict of suicide. This means that whether or not a death gets recorded as suicide is also dependent on suicidal cues that are discovered in the life history of the deceased.

But what sort of additional evidence are the officials looking for when they examine the biography of the deceased? In order to answer this question we have to look at some of the common assumptions that our culture makes about suicide. In western society suicide is a form of deviance but one which we now tend to explain in terms of 'pathology' rather than evil, or moral weakness. We assume that suicide is normally an act of despair and great unhappiness and that this, in turn, is often caused by problems such as mental illness, broken relationships or some other personal crisis.

Research by Atkinson (1978) and myself (1982) has shown that the officials who investigate and categorise sudden deaths tend, by and large, to share these assumptions that are taken for granted about suicide. Thus they work with implict *theories* about the *situations* that are commonly associated wtih suicide and about the kinds of *individuals* who tend to be more vulnerable to suicide in these situations. When officials investigate the biography of someone they suspect might have committed suicide, their assumptions about suicide direct the focus of their attention to particular issues.

1 STATE OF MIND AND BEHAVIOUR PRIOR TO DEATH

Officials want to know how the deceased was behaving during the weeks just before his or her death. They want to know if he or she was particularly unhappy or concerned about something, depressed, or in a 'suicidal' frame of mind. If witnesses provide evidence that the deceased was depressed or very anxious, or had made suicidal threats or previous attempts, then these are significant indicators of suicidal intent.

2 SUICIDAL MOTIVE

Officials also look into the life history of the deceased for evidence that will provide a motive, or explanation, for suicide. Research by **Taylor** (1982) based on interviews and participant observation with coroners and their officers has shown that evidence of a breakdown in a close personal relationship; social problems, especially involving loss of status or personal 'failure'; a history of 'instability', especially mental illness and other deviant behaviour; inability to make or maintain close personal relationships and a 'broken home' in childhood are among the most important suicidal cues in this area. When coroners are able to discover this sort of evidence they are more likely to return (or advise a jury to return) a verdict of suicide.

It is important to bear in mind that evidence of, for example, depression or a broken marriage, does not in itself 'prove' suicide. These are cues which suggest suicide. However, such evidence, in conjunction with significant cues from the circumstances of death, can provide officials with powerful and convincing evidence that death was due to suicide.

Testing the influence of biographical evidence

By considering a series of cases where the circumstances of death are more or less the same, we can then examine the influence of these secondary suicidal cues from the biography of the deceased.

Compare the two cases described below. They are reports of the investigations into two cases of sudden, unexplained death.

CASE I

Mr A, a 37-year-old working man, died as a result of injuries received when he fell under a train. Further investigation revealed that he was married with two children and, apparently, in good health. He was in full-time employment. There was no evidence that Mr A was depressed. Witnesses said he was 'quite cheerful', and none of them could suggest any reason why he should want to end his life.

CASE II

Mr B, a 35-year-old unemployed man, died as a result of injuries received when he fell under a train. Further investigation revealed that Mr B had been living alone since his marriage had broken up two years before. He had not been in regular work for several years. Recently, he had been receiving some medical treatment for alcohol dependence and for depression. For the past few weeks he had been failing to keep his hospital appointments. Acquaintances said Mr B had been very upset and depressed when an attempted reconciliation with his wife had not worked out. In the weeks before his death witnesses said he had often talked of wanting to 'end it all'.

From the evidence that has been collected it seems much more likely that Case II would be recorded as suicide. However, the explanation is not to be found in the circumstances of death, which are more or less identical in both cases, but in the apparent differences in the biography. Case I provides neither evidence of depression nor a motive for suicide. In contrast, Case II reveals a variety of secondary cues which, taken together, help to build up a plausible explanation for suicide. We can call this a *suicidal biography*. Mr B had not been in regular work. He had a history of alcoholism and depression, and did not appear to have close personal ties to support him through difficult times. More recently, there was evidence that he was very upset over the failed reconciliation with his wife and that he had been talking of 'ending it all'.

Of course, many cases may not be as seemingly clear cut as the two outlined above. Officials may sometimes find conflicting evidence 'for' and 'against' suicidal intent. However, in the majority of cases where suicide is suspected, it is evidence (or lack of evidence) of intent from the biography of the deceased that is crucial in determining whether or not a verdict of suicide is returned.

In a study of how deaths under London Transport underground trains were recorded (Taylor, 1982), I took 32 cases from the total sample. In these cases the circumstances of death were more or less identical in every respect: 17 (53.1 per cent) were recorded as suicides. What distinguished the 'suicidal' from the 'non-suicidal' group was biographical evidence from which the coroner could reconstruct an appropriately 'suicidal biography'. This enabled the coroner to make the verdict consistent with general cultural assumptions about suicide.

Implications for suicide research

We have seen that, even when there is a strong suggestion of suicide from the circumstances of death, a suicide verdict will normally only be brought in when there is sufficient evidence of intent from the biography of the deceased. It is this biographical and social evidence which is likely to *introduce important sources of systematic bias into the official suicide rates*. It will be useful to look at a specific example in some detail to illustrate this important general point.

We have observed how officials attach great importance to the deceased's state of mind and behaviour just prior to death. In particular, they want to know if he or she was depressed, talking about suicide and so on. To a certain extent, this area of evidence is *negotiated* by the coroner and witnesses. The outcome is often dependent on who gives this evidence. When an individual has been in a relatively 'integrated', or family, situation just before his death, evidence of how he was behaving is normally given by one or more of his significant others – that is, those with whom he had close personal ties. However, if the deceased has been away from his family for some time, or does not have close personal ties, evidence will be given by witnesses more distant to him; for example, neighbours, colleagues, a doctor or social worker.

A coroner will normally ask witnesses if they can think of any reason why the deceased might have wanted to commit suicide. Witnesses will either tend to confirm or refute the suggestion of suicide. When this evidence is given by significant others of the deceased, it is much more likely that attempts will be made to refute the suggestion of suicide. Also, significant others are normally in a better position to suggest reasons why the deceased could not have wished to commit suicide; they can point out that he or she was 'always cheerful', 'really looking forward to a new job' and so on.

The results of the London Transport study tend to confirm the hypothesis that evidence of suicidal intent from the behaviour of the deceased is less likely to be forthcoming when it was given by the deceased's significant others. The study also showed that when evidence of intent was not forthcoming at this stage of the inquiry, there was less likelihood of a suicide verdict being returned.

These observations have important implications for the traditional sociological approach to suicide. Sociological studies from Durkheim onwards have consistently found an inverse relationship between social integration and suicide. That is, the suicide statistics show that low rates of social integration are associated with a high rate of suicide and vice versa. However, investigation into the social construction of official suicide rates provides another explanation of the same consistent statistical relationship. This research suggests that social integration has an important biasing influence on both the recognition and recording of suicide.

We can apply essentially the same arguments to many other findings of the study of suicide rates. This body of work has shown that suicide is positively and consistently related to factors such as social isolation, status loss, social problems, marital breakdown, mental illness, alcoholism and social deviance and a broken home in childhood. However, we have seen that when evidence of such factors in the deceased's biography is discovered, this can help to provide officials with a socially acceptable motive, or explanation, for suicide. On the other hand, when such evidence does not emerge from investigation of the biography, then, in spite of what the officials themselves might believe, a suicide verdict is unlikely to be returned.

Research into the way in which official suicide rates are socially produced shows that the official figures not only under-estimate the volume of suicide (something most researchers accept anyway), but also that there are *systematic biases* in the official statistics which mean that they are an *unrepresentative* sample of the whole. This, of course, is not necessarily the end of the story. Future research (or changes in collection procedures) may point us in other directions. However, in relation to the research problem that we posed at the beginning of this chapter, the research examined here suggests that a *sceptical* view of official suicide rates is more appropriate than a position of *acceptance*, and that we must apply this scepticism to our analysis of the work of Durkheim and other sociological (and non-sociological) studies of suicide rates.

Summary

This chapter has been concerned with the social processes by which some deaths come to be labelled as suicides. First, from the immediate circumstances, the death must 'look like' a suicide. That is, it must resemble society's expectations of the ways in which men and women kill themselves in western society. Secondly, there must be evidence of suicidal intent in the deceased's biography in order to 'justify' a verdict of suicide.

It has been argued here that the social processes, negotiations, legal and bureaucratic constraints involved in this procedure introduce systematic sources of bias into the official suicide rates which suggest that they are unacceptable for research purposes. Thus, when researchers study the official suicide rates and find suicide consistently and positively related to factors such as social isolation, status loss, social problems and deviance, it is possible that they are discovering, not factors associated with the causes of suicide, but rather the criteria used by officials to infer suicidal intent.

Some of the arguments that we have raised in relation to suicide rates can also be applied to other sets of official statistics. However, this should not be taken to imply that we should necessarily reject statistical materials and advocate 'qualitative' as opposed to 'quantitative' methodologies. The important thing for the researcher is to show that a set of statistics fulfils the function assigned to it. In the case of suicide statistics the research evidence suggests this is not the case. This does not mean that sociological theories of suicide based on the statistics are necessarily wrong, or that we should abandon the idea that suicidal behaviour is related to social influences, but it does mean that these theories (and the fundamental idea that suicide is a product of society) have not been 'demonstrated' as convincingly as their authors sometimes assert. Durkheim, for example, claimed that the truth of his theory had been 'proved' by the suicide statistics. Having studied the social construction of official suicide rates, we are in a better position to question that claim. It also gives rise to the question of the alternative ways in which sociologists have tried to study suicide, and this is what we examine in the following chapter.

5 Interpretive approaches to suicide

Interpretive sociology

In the sociology of suicide the main alternative to the traditional sociological approach comes from those who favour a more interpretive, or subjectivist, approach to the study of social life. Although there are different approaches within interpretive sociology, it is possible to identify certain common assumptions made by interpretive sociologists.

Interpretive sociology rejects the positivists' notion of a single, unified scientific method. It claims that there are significant differences between the study of the natural world and the study of the social world. Human beings engage in conscious, intentional activity and, through language, they attach *meanings* to their actions. What we call 'society' is the product of the meaningful interaction between individuals. We have already observed in Chapter 4 how interpretive sociologists stressed the importance of examining the definitions that coroners and other officials hold about suicide. Similarly, they have argued that the first task in 'understanding' suicide is to examine the meanings that suicidal individuals 'construct' for their actions and that, as far as possible, these meanings should be understood in terms of the immediate social contexts from which they emerge.

Interpretive sociology thus has a preference for research methodologies, such as participant observation, 'depth' interviews, case records and other types of personal documents, that bring the researcher as close as possible to the world of the subjects that he or she is studying. The famous Chicago School of sociology, which favoured this approach and sent its researchers out exploring every corner of the city, claimed that the aim of research was to 'tell it as it is'.

'Societal reaction' theory

One avenue within the interpretive approach to suicide is the application of the interactionist, or societal reaction, perspective.

From this point of view, a key factor in causing suicidal behaviour is the *reaction of others* to a potentially suicidal individual. The focus is therefore on the interpersonal relations of the situation. **W. Rushing** (in *Deviant Behaviour and Social Process*, 1975), for example, observes that a suicide, or suicide attempt, is often preceded by deviant behaviour such as alcoholism or drug abuse, or by economic or social failure. A person who is labelled as deviant is more likely to receive negative or stigmatising reactions from others. This tends both to lower the individual's sense of self-esteem and weaken his or her social relationships with other people, which then makes the possibility of suicide more likely.

A more detailed research example of the societal reaction approach to suicide is found in **A. Kobler and E. Stotland's** book *The End of Hope* (1964). This is the study of an outbreak of suicides ('suicide epidemic') in a mental hospital. The patients concerned had come to see the hospital treatment as their last hope of recovery. Kobler and Stotland argue that the unintentionally negative responses the patients received from a very demoralised staff to their desperate cries for help and hope was crucial in triggering the 'epidemic'. In Kobler and Stotland's view, suicide is preceded by two things. First, the individual must define himself or herself as helpless to remedy his or her misery; and second, he or she perceives others (intentionally or unintentionally) defining the situation as hopeless. In this context Kobler and Stotland observe that it was perhaps ironic that the introduction of new 'suicide precautions' in the hospital unintentionally helped to convey this sense of hopelessness to some patients by providing an 'implicit expectation that the troubled person will kill himself'.

By focusing on the importance of the reaction of others to the potentially suicidal individual, the societal reaction approach has highlighted an important and relatively neglected element of the suicide process. However, such an approach is better conceived as a contribution to our understanding of suicide rather than being, in itself, an 'alternative approach'. First, we still have to explain why some individuals become 'helpless' and potentially suicidal, and secondly, we still have to show why negative labelling produces a 'suicidal' response in some but not in others.

Neo-phenomenology

Other students who adopt an interpretive viewpoint argue that the researcher must, as far as possible, begin without preconceived ideas and assumptions about suicide. The initial aim should be to identify, or empathise, with the subject's experiences rather than try to explain his or her behaviour. We call this approach neo-phenomenological.

J. Jacobs (in *Social Problems* 15, 1967) has criticised Durkheim and most other sociologists who have studied suicide rates for assuming that they could explain suicide by bypassing the study of the suicidal individual. He argues that understanding of suicide can *only* 'emerge' from detailed consideration of how the suicidal individual defines the situation. Suicide notes provide a good source of data because they throw some light on the important question of how the subject justifies (to himself or herself and others) the decision to commit suicide and break the sacred trust of life. From his study of suicide notes, Jacobs argues that in order to do this the individual must first feel he is faced with an intolerable and unsolvable problem; secondly, believe that death is the only answer; and thirdly, be able to define the situation as being beyond his control. Jacobs claims that the majority of the 112 notes he studied illustrate this process to a greater or lesser extent.

Jacobs's study draws attention to the researcher 'taking seriously what the suicidal person writes in attempting to explain to the survivors why he is commiting suicide'. Of course, in its present form, the study has fairly obvious limitations. First, suicide notes are discovered only in a minority of cases and, even then, they are often too short and ambiguous to allow any conclusions to be drawn from them. It could be, therefore, that those who write fairly long notes are a selective rather than a random sample of suicidal cases (see pages 24–25). Secondly, analysis is restricted to one aspect of the suicide process, that is, how the suicidal individual *justifies* the action. It does not begin to explain why some individuals find themselves in that situation in the first place.

Douglas's work on suicide (1967) is often seen as the most comprehensive attempt to create an interpretive alternative to the traditional sociological approach to suicide. He argues that the sociologist's first task should be a detailed analysis of the 'situated', or concrete, meanings of particular suicidal acts through, for example, interviews with 'survivors', case reports, diaries and other documentary sources. The next task is to look for recurring patterns, or dimensions, of meaning. Douglas calls these the social meanings of suicide. He argues that some of the most common of these meanings include 'revenge', 'the search for help', 'escape', 'repentance' and 'seriousness'.

Douglas argues that the social meanings that a culture holds about suicide can have an important bearing on the meaning that an individual 'constructs' for a suicidal act. For example, the idea in the modern western world that suicide means that there is something drastically wrong with the individual and that people can be 'driven' to this desperate situation, means that a person can use suicide to indicate that others are to blame for this state of affairs. In other words, suicide can be used to inflict 'revenge' on others. Douglas uses the following case to illustrate this social meaning of suicide.

> A young clerk 22 years old killed himself because his bride of four months was not in love with him but with his elder brother and wanted a divorce so she could marry the brother. The letters he left showed plainly the suicide's desire to bring unpleasant notoriety upon his brother and his wife, and to attract attention to himself. In them he described his shattered romance and advised reporters to see a friend to whom he had forwarded diaries for further details. The first sentence in a special message to his wife read: 'I used to love you; but I die hating you and my brother too.' . . . Still another note read, 'To whom it may interest: The cause of it all: I loved and trusted my wife and trusted my brother. Now I hate my wife and despise my brother and sentence myself to die for having been fool enough to ever have loved anyone as contemptible as my wife has proven to be.' . . . The day before his death, there was a scene and when assured that the two were really deeply in love with each other, the clerk retorted: 'All right, I can do you more harm dead than alive.'
>
> (J. Douglas, *The Social Meanings of Suicide*, Princeton University Press, 1967)

Developing Douglas's approach, **J. Baechler** (1979) has argued that suicidal behaviour, rather than being simply an end, is a means, or a strategy, by which people seek to achieve particular ends. The crucial question, therefore, is what problems are people trying to resolve when they resort to suicide. From his analysis of a wide range of case material, Baechler argues that there are four types of general meaning of suicidal behaviour: (1) *escapist*, where suicide is used to flee from an intolerable situation; (2) *aggressive*, where the subject intends to harm or appeal to others; (3) *oblative*, directed towards some political or moral ideal; and (4) *ludic*, where the subject is gambling with life and death. (The gambling aspect of suicidal behaviour will be discussed in the following chapter.)

In summary, the interpretive approach has made an important contribution to the sociology of suicide. Not only has it helped to provide a valuable critique of official suicide rates, but it has also made particular contributions to the understanding of individual experiences of suicide.

Comparison of two sociological approaches to suicide

We have looked at two different approaches to the sociological study of suicide; what we have called the traditional sociological approach and the interpretive approach. We are now in a position to compare the two and note some of their strengths and limitations. The traditional sociological approach begins by studying suicide in its collective form – that is, by observing and attempting to explain the general distribution of suicide in given populations. Interpretive sociologists like Jacobs, Douglas and Baechler take more or less the opposite route. They argue that sociology must begin with the study of particular suicidal actions – what Douglas calls 'real world' suicidal actions – before moving outwards and grouping similar types of cases together. The main differences between the two approaches are summarised in Table 5.1 (see page 44).

It is not simply a question of choosing which approach is 'right' and which one is 'wrong'. Each approach tends to emphasise only aspects of the problem of suicide. As we have seen, the interpretive approach tries to 'reinstate' the subject. It stresses the importance of studying the subject's definition of the situation.

Some critics claim that interpretive research is too dependent on the subject's view, that it is impressionistic, lacking in objectivity, and that it does not allow for the testing of specific hypotheses. In response to this kind of criticism some interpretive sociologists have argued that, as the case of official statistics

Table 5.1   *Comparison between traditional and interpretive approaches*

	Stage I	*Stage II*	*Stage III*
Traditional sociological approach	Examine the general distribution of suicide in given populations.	Explore and explain the relationship between patterns of suicide and social influences.	Explain and illustrate the influence of social causes on individual acts of suicide.
Interpretive approach	Document individual experiences of suicide in as much detail as possible.	Look for recurring patterns to identify types of suicidal behaviour.	Examine the relationship between types of individual suicidal actions and wider social influences.

shows, for example, the 'objectivity' of 'scientific' sociology is more apparent than real. They claim that, because social life is about human experiences, or subjectivity, the social sciences cannot hope to match the objectivity of the natural sciences.

It should be made clear that Table 5.1 illustrates aims and ideals for each approach. In practice the traditional sociological approach has told us little about individual suicide – how, to use Durkheim's terms, the social forces that cause suicide become 'individualised'. Similarly, the interpretive approach has told us correspondingly little about some of the ways in which individual experiences of suicide are influenced by wider society. This is an important point. The discipline of sociology is founded on the assumption that individual actions are shaped to a greater or lesser extent by the nature of collective social life or society. Thus the criticism that interpretive sociology does not attempt to make clear enough the relationship of the individual to the collectivity – which certainly has some justification as far as interpretive studies of suicide are concerned – is one that must be taken seriously.

It should not be assumed that the traditional and interpretive are the only sociological approaches to suicide. Other sociological perspectives, such as 'learning theory' and 'exchange theory', have been applied to the study of suicide, while some positivist sociologists have studied case histories in preference to suicide rates. We have compared the traditional and interpretive approaches only because these are the dominant approaches in the sociology of suicide and provide us with some of the best insights towards explaining the problem. Also, we have used the example of the study of suicide to illustrate more general theoretical and methodological debates within sociology. Many of these debates are not new, but are as old as sociology itself. For example, at the end of the last century Durkheim was criticising those 'individualists' who argued that society was the *product* of individual actions based on choice, or free will. As we have seen, Durkheimian sociology was an attempt to demonstrate the extent to which the individual was constrained by society. Yet only a few years ago we find **J. Baechler** (*Suicides*, 1979) strongly critical of Durkheim and advocating a 'new approach' based on the assumption that 'men make their own destinies'.

These continuing debates represent unresolved tensions in sociology, but this does not mean that research is doomed to go round in circles and fail to develop and progress. In the following chapter we shall illustrate this general point by looking at a weakness that was common both to traditional and interpretive approaches to suicide. We shall then show how more recent research is attempting to remedy this problem.

Summary and conclusions

In this chapter we have looked at the interpretive approach to suicide and compared it to the traditional approach. The interpretive view places much more weight on the examination of the suicidal individual and the meanings that he or she gives to the suicidal act. However, interpretive studies of suicide (as illustrated by the work of Douglas, for example) tend to be less than clear as to how sociology is to make the leap from the study of 'individual' meanings of suicide to shared, or general, patterns of meanings of suicidal acts and how these meanings are influenced by society.

It was also observed that there were certain weaknesses in both approaches. In particular, works on suicide by sociologists have tended to be confined to completed, or fatal, suicide. Sociologists have generally made little attempt to study the many suicidal actions that do not end in death, nor have they examined in much detail the situations in which people harm themselves. As a result of these omissions, sociologists (and others) have tended to accept certain mistaken 'common-sense' assumptions about suicide. They have employed a definition, or concept, of suicide that does little justice to the complexities of suicidal behaviour, and prevents fuller explanation of the problem. What then do we mean by a suicidal act? And what errors have sociologists tended to make in the way that they have defined suicide? It is to these problems that we turn in the next chapter.

6 The social context of suicidal actions

Suicide and risk taking

This section is concerned with the problem of what we mean by a suicidal act. The answer may seem perfectly simple. Suicide is an intentional act of self-killing. Most sociologists have defined suicide in these terms. Durkheim (*Suicide*, 1952), for example, defined suicide as a term 'applied to all cases of death resulting directly or indirectly from a positive or negative act of the victim himself which he knows will produce this result. An attempt is an act thus defined but falling short of actual death.'

It is recognised, of course, that there are those who 'fake', or 'play', at suicide, but sociologists have tended to assume that a clear distinction can be made between the 'genuine' suicide act (where the individual really wants to die) and various other 'non-suicidal' acts, such as suicidal gestures (where the individual really wants to live). This common-sense view of suicide would recognise the following distinctions outlined in Table 6.1.

Table 6.1   Common-sense view of suicide

Suicide:	Individual intends to die and does die.
Attempted suicide:	Individual intends to die, but fails to do so.
Suicidal gesture:	Individual has no real intention of dying and does not do so.
Accident:	Individual does not intend to die but, due to unforeseen circumstances, does die.

This common-sense view of suicide seems quite logical. However, when we look at the situations in which, and methods by which, people deliberately harm themselves – what we call the micro-social contexts of suicide – the distinction between the 'genuine' suicidal act and the 'fake' suicidal act is not nearly so clear. Consider the following cases:

CASE I

She had made several dangerous attempts before. She poisoned herself with narcotics in her home during the night. There were no signs of precautions against survival. On the contrary, her housekeeper was at home and might easily have come into her bedroom before it was too late. [She] was found dead clutching the telephone. Shortly before she took the poison she had a talk with her doctor over the phone telling him of her depression and anxiety. She had been in the habit of doing this, with or without suicidal threats. On many previous occasions the doctor had come to her house during the night and managed to calm her down. That particular night he tried to do so by talking to her over the phone. . . . He was criticised for not having gone to her house on that occasion as he had often done previously. It is easy to understand that if a patient becomes too demanding appeals for help tend to lose their alarming effect.

CASE II

A man ingested barbiturates and went to sleep in his car which was parked in front of his estranged wife's house. A note to her was pinned on his chest indicating his expectation that she would notice him when she returned from her date with another man. This possibility of being rescued, however, was obliterated by a dense fog which descended around midnight.

CASE III

She became very depressed after her marriage of fifteen years broke up and was being prescribed anti-depressants. One morning at work she began swallowing the tablets one by one. A colleague at work noticed what she was doing and reported it to a senior. The company doctor was called in and he summoned an ambulance. She was unconscious on arrival at hospital, but survived, after intensive medical treatment. She later said that she was unsure about her intentions at the time she was taking the tablets.

CASE IV

Now with the revolver in my pocket I thought I had stumbled on the perfect cure. I was going to escape in one way or another. . . . The discovery that it was possible to enjoy again the visible world by risking its total loss was one I was bound to make sooner or later.

I put the muzzle of the revolver to my right ear and pulled the trigger. There was a minute click, and looking down the chamber I could see that the charge had moved into the firing position. I was out by one. I remember an extraordinary sense of jubilation, as if carnival lights had been switched on in a dark drab street. My heart knocked in its cage and life contained an infinite number of possibilities.

Are the four cases described above genuine suicide attempts or mere gestures which, in two cases, 'misfired' and ended in actual death? None of them appears to fit comfortably into either category. In each case there was the possibility of death, yet in none of them was death more or less inevitable. It appears that the individuals involved in these cases were *risking* their lives. They were *gambling* with life and death.

Of course, not all suicidal acts follow this behaviour pattern. There are those who do wholeheartedly seek death through suicide and try to take precautions against failing, and there are those who make suicidal gestures where the situation is manipulated so there is virtually no chance of death. However, research by psychiatrists and others into the situations in which people deliberately and seriously harm themselves – the microsocial context of suicidal actions – has consistently shown that the vast majority of suicidal acts fall *between these extremes*. For example, two Swedish psychiatrists, **R. Ettlinger and P. Flordah** (in *Acta Psychiatrica*, 1955) made a detailed study of the social situations in which 500 cases of serious deliberate self-harm took place. They estimated that, while only 4 per cent of their sample could be called 'planned' in the sense that precautions were taken against being discovered, in their view only 7 per cent were more or less 'harmless' in the sense that there was little or no chance of the individual dying. Thus in the vast majority of cases – almost 90 per cent – there was the risk of death with chance factors determining whether or not the individual lived or died. A number of other researchers, including **E. Stengel, J. Weiss**, and **S. Taylor** have similarly concluded that the majority of serious suicidal acts, including many that actually end in death, are in fact gambles with death where the 'outcome' is decided by factors outside the individual's control.

Understanding of this characteristic of suicidal behaviour owes most to the pioneering work of Erwin Stengel, late Professor of Psychiatry at Sheffield University. E. Stengel and N. Cook

(*Attempted Suicide*, 1958) made a number of studies of the micro-social contexts of suicidal actions. Stengel did not simply confine his attentions to the suicidal act itself, but reconstructed events prior to the suicidal act and examined the social setting in which it took place. We can refer to this as studying the *suicide process*.

From his research, Stengel reached an interesting and rather paradoxical conclusion. He found that the suicide process, as well as being directed towards death and dying, was also in most cases directed towards *life and survival*. He therefore referred to the suicidal act as being 'Janus-faced' – Janus being a mythological god with two faces pointing in opposite directions.

By definition, suicide is about death and dying, but what characteristics of the suicide process led Stengel to claim that it is also about life and survival? Stengel based his argument on a number of features of the suicide process. For example, in the vast majority of suicidal actions the individual gives a number of warnings and threats to others regarding his or her intentions. Sometimes these are direct warnings of suicidal intent; in other cases the individual may give more indirect 'suicidal clues', such as continual references towards death and dying, giving away treasured possessions and generally 'putting one's house in order', or obscure last-minute telephone calls to friends 'just to say goodbye'.

Often, whether or not the individual lives or dies depends on recognition of, and action taken in response to, the warnings and threats or other 'suicidal clues' that are given out. (Have a look again at Case I on page 48.) Also, most suicidal acts are under-taken in a setting (most often a house where other people are present or are likely to be present) and employ a method (most usually poisoning) that makes intervention and rescue a possibility.

It would be wrong to conclude from this that, just because an individual does not try to 'make sure' of dying, he or she is 'not serious' and only 'faking' a suicide attempt. Stengel argues that many who deliberately harm themselves in a suicidal manner are genuinely uncertain as to whether or not they want to go on living. He states:

> Most people who commit acts of self damage with more or less conscious self-destructive intent do not want either to live or to die, but to do both at the same time – usually one more

than the other. . . . Most suicidal acts are manifestations of risk-taking behaviour. They are gambles.

(E. Stengel, 'A Matter of Communication' in E. Shneidman (ed.), *On the Nature of Suicide*, San Francisco, Jossey Bass, 1969)

Research evidence from other sources would seem to support this conclusion. For example, **M. Kovacs and A. Beck** (in *Journal of Clinical Psychology* 33, 1977) found that half their sample of suicide attempters said that they wanted both to live and die at the time of the attempt, while **J. Weiss** (in *Psychiatry* 20, 1957) found that 113 out of a sample of 156 suicide attempters said that they were uncertain as to whether or not they would die at the time of the attempt.

Stengel (*Suicide and Attempted Suicide*, 1973) has argued that many suicidal acts may be likened to the medieval idea of the ordeal. This was a dangerous test, or trial, to which an individual was submitted to find out whether or not God wanted him or her to live or die. In modern societies some people impose suicidal ordeals on themselves. They risk their lives in order to find out whether or not they are 'meant' to go on living. This ordeal character of suicide is clearly illustrated in the following case quoted by Baechler:

> Mrs C. Paule, 42. Found in a coma in a wood near to where she was a nurse. Suicide with gardenal and insulin. Upon recovering consciousness it appeared to her that she did not think she would truly die; at least, knowing there was a chance that she would survive, she hoped to take advantage of it. She was aware of the incoherence of her behaviour but untroubled by it. 'I sensed myself close to death, but I thought I would live.' She recognised that her attempt displayed aspects of an ordeal.
>
> (J. Baechler, *Suicides*, Blackwell, 1979)

Explaining suicidal behaviour

The observation that the majority of suicidal acts are risk taking and may be likened to medieval ordeals has important implications for our attempts to explain suicide generally and for the sociology of suicide in particular. We have seen how most sociological studies have failed to appreciate the complexities of suicidal behaviour, especially its communicative and risk-taking dimensions. This has led sociologists into accepting a 'common-sense' view of suicide that makes the fundamental error of assuming that all serious suicidal acts are aimed at death alone. As we observed in the previous section, the majority of suicidal acts fall between these extremes. In order to begin to explain this type of behaviour we need a rather broader concept of suicide than the one employed by Durkheim and other sociologists. A suicidal act may, therefore, be defined as any deliberate act of self-damage, or potential self-damage, where the individual cannot be sure of survival.

This view of suicidal behaviour raises rather different questions from the simple and traditional one of why people kill themselves. We must now ask, for example, why so many people risk their lives in a manner similar to a medieval ordeal. And what is the relationship between this type of behaviour and more whole-hearted and single-minded attempts to end life?

I explored these issues in an earlier work, *Durkheim and the Study of Suicide* (1982), by adapting the *basis* of Durkheim's theory of suicide but employing a case-study approach. We have already observed (in Chapter 3) how Durkheim's *realist* approach differed from later nominalist and positivistic studies of suicide rates. It is relevant here to note another important distinction between Durkheim's explanation and that of most other sociologists. Unlike most theorists, who see deviance as caused by 'alien' traits in societies or individuals, Durkheim saw *both deviant and normal behaviour arising from the same sources*. In Durkheim's theory, individuals were 'protected' from suicide by a *balance* between integration and regulation. It was *under*-integration or -regulation or *over*-integration or -regulation that made individuals more vulnerable to suicide (see Figure 6.1).

Using the same *form* of approach, but employing the concept of suicide explained above, it was argued that for an individual to live 'normally' (that is, without thoughts of suicide), there must be in that person's life a *balance* between *certainty* (a sense of stability and predictability about life events) and *uncertainty* (the possibility of change and the unexpected). An excess on either side will leave the individual more vulnerable to suicide. Thus the hypothesis was advanced that 'suicide is more

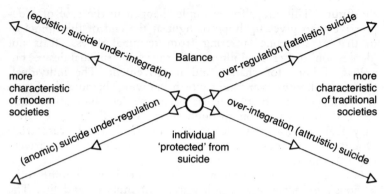

Figure 6.1 Dynamics of Durkheim's theory of suicide

likely in situations of complete uncertainty where the individual feels he or she knows nothing worth knowing, or in situations of complete certainty where the individual feels he or she knows everything worth knowing.'

Suicides resulting from a profound sense of psychological uncertainty will be ordeals. Sometimes the individual is tormented by seemingly unresolvable doubts about self and identity; but, more commonly, he or she is profoundly uncertain about others or, more specifically, the meaning that he or she has for others. In these latter cases, which I call appeals, the individual imposes a suicidal ordeal on himself or herself in order to try to *communicate* desperation and despair to others, or a specific significant other, when all other means of communication appear to have failed. We shall illustrate this in more detail with case-study examples in Part 3, but for the moment the important thing to grasp is that the underlying characteristic of ordeal suicides is that the individual is faced by an uncertainty (about himself or herself or others) which is so intolerable that he or she feels it is impossible to continue living until it is resolved.

Existence, therefore, becomes problematic; that is, the individual wishes to be dead and yet remain alive, and demands a 'judgment' from death to find out if he or she is intended to go on living.

In contrast, there are suicidal acts resulting from the individual's sense of certainty that life is intolerable and will get no better in the future. This may, for example, happen in the case of a depressive who gives up hope of light at the end of the tunnel or in that of someone suffering from terminal illness. It is not 'depression' or 'terminal illness' that causes the suicidal desires but a loss of hope for change and improvement. The individual, therefore, 'knows everything worth knowing' because the future is drained of possibility, all has been revealed. Individuals may come to this realisation through their own reflections, or they may feel (as, for example, in the 'revenge' suicide case from Douglas's work described on page 42) that others have 'driven' them to this state of mind.

Suicidal acts resulting from a sense of certainty are going to be 'serious', or purposive, wholehearted attempts to end life. The individual is not 'playing a game' with death in order to discover whether or not he or she is to remain alive. Rather, he or she is embracing death from a firm conviction that nothing further remains in life.

It is important to emphasise that certainty and uncertainty are not in themselves causes of suicide. All of us in our lives are faced by certainty (the known) and uncertainty (the unknown). It is the *excess* of uncertainty (or certainty) which pushes people towards seeking a suicidal solution to their problems. It must also be made clear that the distinction between ordeal and purposive suicide is not the same as the distinction between attempted and completed suicide. While suicidal ordeals can be lethal, some purposive suicidal acts can in fact be relatively harmless if, for example, the individual is very old or weak. This approach to suicide is summarised in Figure 6.2.

Summary and conclusions

In Part 2 we have examined the major issues in the sociology of suicide. The concern of sociologists – whatever approach they have taken – has been to show that even such a 'private' and self-contained act as suicide exhibits patterns, or regularities, that can be explained sociologically. Durkheim's study of suicide rates laid down a model, or framework, for a particular approach to suicide which we have called the traditional sociological approach. It argues that sociology must begin by studying suicide rates and

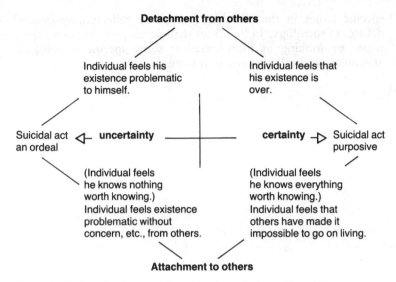

Source: S. Taylor, *Durkheim and the Study of Suicide*, Macmillan, 1982

Figure 6.2 Relationship between ordeal and purposive suicidal acts

explaining their regularities in terms of differing conditions of social life.

Two major questions have been raised about this method of studying suicide. First, there is the question of the reliability of official suicide rates. We examined this in Chapter 4, and considered an alternative explanation of the regularity of suicide rates in terms of the collection procedures of the organisations which categorise 'unnatural deaths'. Second, critics (both inside and outside sociology) have questioned sociology's ability to explain suicide without studying those who actually harm, or try to harm, themselves. In relation to this issue we considered the interpretive approach to suicide, which begins by trying to understand the meaning that a suicidal act has for the individual concerned. We then moved on to the study of the micro-social contexts of suicidal actions. It was observed that sociologists have tended to work with certain mistaken assumptions about suicide, in particular the view that all serious suicidal acts are aimed at death alone. At each stage the attempt was made to show how specific issues in the sociology of suicide reflect more general debates in sociology. In Part 3 we shall develop discussion of these issues by looking in more detail at some specific sociological arguments and relevant research material.

Suicide research: issues and sources

7 Suicide statistics

Suicide rates in England and Wales

Official mortality statistics show that each year in England and Wales approximately 4,000 people take their own lives. Not only is this suicide rate relatively low for a developed country (see Table 7.1), but it has also begun to decline in recent years (see Figure 7.1).

Table 7.1 International suicide rates per 100,000 population

Country	Year	All	Male	Female
Hungary	1977	40.3	56	25.5
Germany (GDR)	1974	36.2	46	27.7
Finland	1975	25	40.6	10.4
Denmark	1977	24.3	30.9	17.8
Austria	1977	24.3	34.8	14.9
Switzerland	1977	23.9	34	14.3
Germany (FED)	1977	22.7	30.2	15.8
Czechoslovakia	1975	21.9	32.5	11.8
Sweden	1977	19.7	28.3	11.2
Japan	1977	17.9	22	13.8
Belgium	1976	16.6	22.1	11.4
France	1976	15.8	22.9	9
Bulgaria	1977	14.4	20.7	8.1
USA	1976	12.5	18.7	6.7
Canada	1975	12.4	17.9	6.8
Poland	1976	12.1	20.6	4
Norway	1977	11.4	16.9	5.9
Australia	1977	11.1	16	6.2
Iceland	1977	10.4	17	3.6

Table 7.1 (continued)

Country	Year	All	Male	Female
New Zealand	1976	9.3	12.6	5.9
Netherlands	1977	9.2	11.5	6.9
England and Wales	1978	8.2	10.2	6.3
Scotland	1977	8.1	9.8	6.5
Israel	1977	6.5	8.2	4.8
Northern Ireland	1977	4.6	5	4.1
Spain	1975	3.9	5.9	2
Greece	1976	2.8	3.8	1.8

Source: WHO statistics, 1980

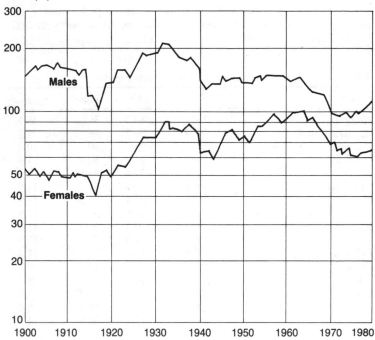

Source: Registrar General

Figure 7.1 Suicide rates per million, by sex, in England and Wales, 1901–78

The official statistics are not just used as a 'measure' of the volume of suicide in a given population, but they also indicate which groups are most vulnerable to suicide. For example, the statistics show that more men than women commit suicide and that the risk of suicide tends to rise with increasing age (Table 7.2).

Table 7.2   Suicide rates per 100,000 in England and Wales, by age and sex, 1963–70

| Age (years) | Men | | | Women | | |
	Rate 1963	1970	% Change	Rate 1963	1970	% Change
15–24	6.9	6	−13	3.1	2.6	−16
25–44	14	10	−29	9.6	5.9	−39
45–64	26	16	−38	17	12	−29
65–74	34	21	−38	20	15	−25
75+	39	24	−38	18	9.7	−46
All ages	14	9.5	−32	9.9	6.6	−33

Source: British Journal of Psychiatry 124, 1974

Sociologists, of course, are particularly interested in the relationships between rates of suicide and other *social* variables, such as social class, family status, religious and ethnic affiliation. In this context it is very important to remember that sociologists are not simply using social variables to help explain suicide, they are also using suicide rates and other demographic data to make general statements about different types of social life.

Deliberate self-harm

If suicide rates in the United Kingdom have been relatively low and declining in recent years, why is self-injury seen as such a problem? The answer is to be found in the dramatic rise in serious, but non-fatal, acts of deliberate self-harm (Table 7.3).

Of course, not all the overdose cases that reach hospital are full-blooded, 'unsuccessful' attempts to end life; the majority are undertaken with confused, ambivalent intentions (see Chapter 6). Nevertheless, in most cases there is severe risk to life, and the drain on the over-worked medical services is immense. It has been estimated that 20 per cent of all emergency hospital beds are

Table 7.3   Hospital admissions for adverse effects of poisons

	Adverse effects of medicinal agents	*Adverse effects of substances chiefly non-medicinal*	*Total*
1961	23,900	4,500	28,400
1962	28,700	5,400	34,100
1963	39,000	7,400	46,400
1964	42,900	8,100	51,000
1965	45,600	8,600	54,200
1966	50,300	9,500	59,800
1967	57,200	10,800	68,000
1968	62,320	12,130	74,450
1969	75,550	14,570	90,120
1970	79,160	14,020	93,180
1971	85,370	14,510	99,880
1972	91,440	14,280	105,720
1973	92,970	14,200	107.170
1974	98,290	14,870	113.160
1975	105,290	15,080	120.370
1976	108,210	17,030	125,240
1977	106,710	14,740	121,450

Source: Hospital Inpatient Enquiry, 1981

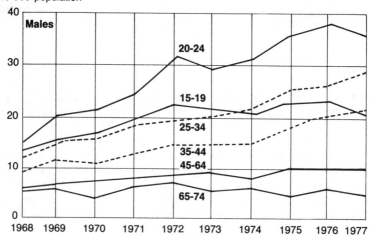

Discharge rate per
10 000 population

occupied by overdose victims. On average, 65 per cent of over-dosers are females, and 25 per cent are females under 25 years old. Indeed, the highest rates of overdose admissions have occurred among young people (see Figure 7.2). While these figures are not subject to the same kind of restraints as suicide rates (for example, the necessity of having to prove suicide in law), we still await detailed sociological analysis into their social construction.

Traditionally, sociologists have tended to confine their attentions to fatal, or completed, suicide and it is only recently that

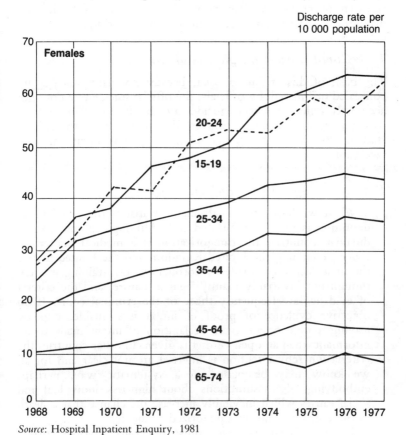

Source: Hospital Inpatient Enquiry, 1981

Figure 7.2 (above and left)   Age-specific hospital discharge rates for adverse reactions to medical agents, England and Wales, 1968–77

they have begun to explore non-fatal suicidal action and the relationship between fatal and non-fatal suicide.

Criticisms of official suicide rates

While official statistics appear to provide a useful index of the levels and nature of suicidal behaviour, we observed in Chapter 4 that there has been considerable questioning of their value for research purposes. We can now take that analysis further by distinguishing between three distinct forms of critique.

1   Positivist critique: the problem of accuracy

The basis of this critique is that, because so many suicides are concealed or 'missed' by officials, the official suicide rate does not accurately reflect the 'real' suicide rate. In the following extract **Morgan** quoting research sources, does not dismiss the suicide statistics, but warns researchers of the danger of taking them at face value.

Reading 1   Official and 'true' suicide rate

When we look at official suicide statistics the problem of definition is more complicated still. Although in some Scandinavian countries the categorization is a medical matter, in others, including the United Kingdom and the United States, the final decision is made by coroners whose training is often though not invariably mainly legal in nature, and the criteria of evidence are frequently those of the criminal court. If no objective evidence of proof of intent is available, e.g. by leaving a note or an overt declaration of intent made to an informant, then an open verdict is given. In other countries the criteria whereby intention is inferred are not clear and for all we know may be biased in a systematic way, perhaps embodying false assumptions about high-risk individual and social causes which inevitably increase the chance that a death in these groups may be categorized a suicide.

To be efficient statistics must not only involve correct categorization based on appropriate definition, but there must also be adequate case detection: we need to know the extent to which cases may be concealed and not reported, how thorough the examination of evidence has been, and to what extent suicides may be missed because of the undoubted tendency to avoid a diagnosis of suicide if doubt exists.

There is a great deal of evidence to suggest that official estimates of suicide lead to a considerable underestimate of its true incidence. McCarthy and Walsh (1975) estimated that in Dublin city and county during the years 1964–1968 the rate of suicide ascertained by psychiatrists' evaluation of medical records was four times greater than that estimated by official coroner's statistics. This problem has also been highlighted by work from the Los Angeles Suicide Prevention Center, where it has been shown that an intensive retrospective evaluation of the total situation surrounding deaths from uncertain causes, including interviews with relatives, may reveal more suicides than those declared through official statistics (Litman *et al.*, 1963).

(H. Morgan, *Death Wishes*, Wiley, 1979, p. 10)

The positivist critique does not question the assumption that suicide can be objectively defined and analysed. Rather, concern is that there are certain technical problems which reduce the reliability of the official statistics. This is outlined in the formula:

'True' suicide rate = Official suicide + unrecognised suicide rate

From this perspective, the solution is to try to produce more *accurate* 'measures' of the true suicide rate. In this context **A. Adelstein and C. Mardon** (in *Population Trends* 2, 1975) have suggested that a more reliable index of suicide will be achieved by adding open verdicts and poisonings recorded as accidental to the official suicide rate. The results of this kind of procedure are illustrated in Figure 7.3 (see pages 64 and 65).

2 Subjectivist critique: the problem of validity

The core of the subjectivist, or interpretive, critique is not that 'real' suicides are being 'missed' but that suicide itself is a product of social definition. The ideas and beliefs that different cultures and subcultures hold about suicide and self-injury determine what is 'seen', and thus classified as 'suicide'. From this perspective the

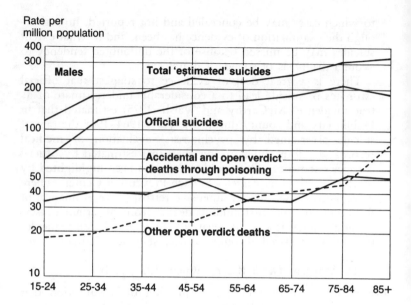

Rate per
million population

suicide statistics may well be 'accurate', in the sense that they reflect what various bureaucracies define and recognise as suicide, but they are not *valid* for the type of research undertaken by Durkheim and others because the meanings of suicide vary both between cultures and within cultures.

Douglas has criticised the traditional sociological approach's use of official suicide rates on precisely these grounds. In the following extract he summarises these objections.

Reading 2   Negotiation of suicide verdicts

The most important error involved in the use of the official statistics, however, has been the same error as that made in the theories themselves; that is, the assumption that 'suicidal actions' have a necessary and sufficient, unidimensional meaning throughout the Western world. This assumption lies behind the assumption (or argument) that the officials must be making use of the same definition as the theorists and that all of the officials must be making use of the same definition. It lies behind the assumption (almost never even made explicit)

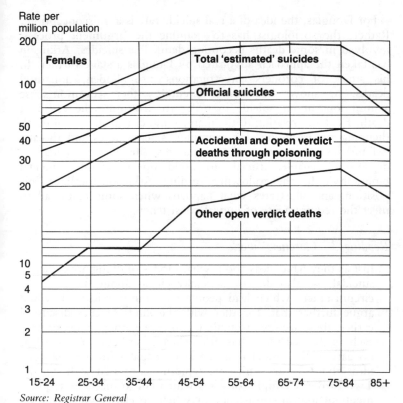

Rate per
million population

Source: Registrar General

*Figure 7.3 (above and left)   Official and estimated suicides by age group,
England and Wales, 1976–77*

that the categorization of a death as 'suicide' would mean the
same thing to all social groups, strata, and individuals, so that
any actions relevant to the official statistics (such as attempts
to hide the facts about the death so that it would not be categorized as a suicide) would be equally distributed throughout
the society being considered. Most significantly, this assumption lies behind the failure to see that an *official* categorization
of the cause of death is as much the end result of an *argument*
as such a categorization by any other member of society.

(J. Douglas, *The Social Meanings of Suicide*, Princeton
University Press, 1967, p. 229)

For Douglas, the idea of a real suicide rate is a 'misconception'. Rather, the sociologist has to examine the 'argument process' involved in some deaths becoming defined as suicides. Atkinson has taken the approach advocated by Douglas a stage further. In his study of coroners' investigations into sudden, unnatural deaths, he shows how officials employ their common-sense assumptions about suicide in order to determine the cause of death. Evidence relating to the manner and circumstances of death (hanging or drowning, for example), suicide notes and threats, 'telling' evidence from the deceased's life history (such as depression) enable officials to build up a suitable 'suicidal biography'. In the following reading Atkinson outlines this position, and illustrates what happens when some cases fail to meet the requirements of logical consistency.

Reading 3   Coroners' work

Just as they have ideas about what modes of dying are typically suicidal, so also do coroners have ideas about the kinds of circumstances which lead people to commit suicide. I would argue further that, together with the kinds of cues discussed earlier, these are used to build up an explanatory model of how each death occurred. Thus, for a suicide verdict to be recorded, no part of the model must be inconsistent with the coroner's ideas about factors which are typically associated with suicide. Two further examples of cases which fail to meet the requirements of logical consistency may help to clarify what I mean:

> CASE 1: A widow aged eighty-five was found gassed in the kitchen of her cottage, where she had lived alone since the death of her husband. Rugs and towels had been stuffed under the door and around the window casements. At the inquest, the few people who knew her testified that she always seemed to be a very happy and cheerful person, and the coroner recorded an open verdict on the grounds that there was no evidence to show how the gas taps had been turned on.

Here, the case appears initially as a clear-cut suicide: a lonely old widow gasses herself taking special precautions to prevent the escape of gas. The evidence that she was apparently perfectly happy, however, must have raised enough doubt in the coroner's mind to lead him away from a suicidal verdict, as happiness is inconsistent with suicidal intent. Putting this another way, one could say that the evidence about her happiness prevented him from explaining satisfactorily why she should have committed suicide. The same thing also seems to apply in this next case:

CASE 2: A seventeen-year-old schoolboy who normally went out shopping with his parents at a certain time on a particular day refused to do so on the day he died, and was thus left alone in the house. When his parents returned, they found him hanging from the banisters on the landing. During the previous two years he had been under regular psychiatric treatment for depression, and was known to be currently worried about what he would do when he left school. At the inquest, a witness testified that he and the boy had been planning a climbing holiday together in the near future, and that a book on climbing had been found open on the deceased's bed at the time of the death. An open verdict was recorded.

Here again, everything initially pointed to a suicide. The method used, the fact that steps had been taken to minimize the chances of intervention, the recurrent depressions and the present worries. The additional evidence, however, raised the possibility of an alternative explanation: he could have been practising climbing and hanged himself accidentally. That the coroners in these two cases had doubts is evidenced by the fact that open verdicts were recorded, as coroners on the whole tend to avoid open verdicts whenever possible. In other words, the evidence in both was not sufficiently consistent to enable them to build up a tenable model of either a suicidal or accidental death.

(J. Atkinson, *Discovering Suicide*, Macmillan, 1978)

3 Rationalist critique: the problem of classification

Although there are obvious and important differences between positivism and subjectivism, they are not mutually exclusive alternatives. Both are examples of a nominalist view of social science which bases knowledge of the world on experience of it (see pages 20–21). In contrast, the realist alternative holds that knowledge of the world is mediated by the organising properties of the human mind. We call this view of knowledge *rationalist*, and we evaluate our understanding in terms of the *logical* relationship between theoretical concepts and empirical events.

Hindess adopts a rationalist position in his discussion of the uses of official statistics in sociology. While he does not accept the positivist view that suicides exist 'out there' waiting to be recognised or not by relevant officials, he is equally critical of the subjectivist position, which he claims, taken to its logical conclusion, denies the possibility of any understanding of the world.

Let us examine this charge in more detail. As we have seen, Douglas and others have argued that we 'see' things in the way we do because of certain underlying assumptions and beliefs which they call 'background expectations'. As a result of these underlying assumptions, certain things come to be defined as 'suicides', 'crimes' or whatever. It is claimed that, by careful observation, detailed interviews and so on, the sociologist can reveal the presence and influence of these background expectations. But what about the sociologist's background expectations? What structures his or her perception of the situation? Surely the sociologist's account is equally 'contaminated' by underlying assumptions? How, then, do we know that the sociologist's account is any more valid than that of the officials whose decisions produce the data? In the following extract Hindess takes up this point and pursues it to its logical conclusions.

Reading 4   The contradiction in the subjectivist position

Douglas, on the other hand, criticises sociologists for their reliance upon observers' descriptions and classifications of phenomena and calls instead for 'careful descriptions of real-world events'.

We have only to ask how the sociologist is to produce his description of 'real-world events' or how he is to communicate 'seen but unnoticed background expectancies' to realise the absurdity of these prescriptions. Unless the sociologist is to be accorded the capacity, denied to ordinary mortals, to describe objects and events without the intervention of background expectancies or of tacit knowledge, then his accounts must be subject to precisely the same type of limitation as those of other observers. In that case his remarks cannot be 'taken on faith as an accurate portrayal of "what happened"'. For every sociologist's account we require a second account of how his background expectancies affected his account. This second account requires a third, and so on. The circularity of the prescribed procedure is obvious. We are faced with an infinite regression at no stage of which is it possible to escape the determination of seen but unnoticed background expectancies. These positions, therefore, lead to a complete relativism and to a necessary agnosticism with respect to the possibility of an objective knowledge of the world. The full significance of these authors' arguments should now be entirely clear. They may be directed against the objectivity of official statistics but they would dispose of the objectivity of all knowledge. What is at stake in these positions is not the utility of this or that lot of data, but the possibility of an objective knowledge of society. (B. Hindess, *The Uses of Official Statistics in Sociology*, Macmillan, 1973, pp. 11–12)

It is very important to note that this line of argument is not opposed to examining the underlying assumptions of officials and the workings of statistics-producing organisations. Rather, it is directed towards exposing the contradiction in the subjectivist critique. Douglas, for example, contrasts the data on suicide produced by officials with what he calls accurate description of 'real world' suicide actions. However, if in principle accurate description is possible, then it is possible to have 'accurate' statistics, which brings the subjectivist position very close to the positivist one it is allegedly criticising.

For the rationalist, official statistics reflect neither the 'objective reality' of suicide, nor the subjectivity of those who compile the data; they are products of the theoretical categories in terms of which they are collected. The crucial question, therefore, is the extent to which there is a correspondence between the researcher's use of some set of statistics and the nature of those statistics.

Conclusion

If we attempt to put these various critical perspectives together we can conclude that any analysis into the quality of a set of official statistics should involve examination of:

1 the theoretical concepts in terms of which the statistics are collected;
2 legal and bureaucratic constraints (for example, the necessity in some countries of having to prove suicide in law);
3 the subjective beliefs, assumptions and so on of the officials who compile the data.

The research evidence documented in Chapter 3 suggested that, in terms of each of these criteria, suicide statistics, for the present at least, should be viewed with extreme caution.

Questions

1 What trends can be identified from examination of the suicide statistics for England and Wales?
2 What do the statistics on admissions for deliberate self-harm tell us?
3 How do Adelstein and Mardon suggest that the official suicide statistics can be made more reliable?
4 Explain the difference between the problem of accuracy and the problem of validity in criticisms of official suicide rates.
5 What does Atkinson mean by the construction of a suitable suicidal biography?
6 Outline the basis of Hindess's criticism of Douglas's position.

8 Sociology and suicide

Introduction

Sociologists have no monopoly in talking about society. As citizens we all learn about our society simply by participating in it. Furthermore, there are people such as politicians, church leaders, journalists and other 'experts' only too willing to tell us more about our society, what is wrong with it and what can and should be done to improve it. This raises the question of what is *distinctive* about a sociologist's view. Durkheim believed that, in order to justify its existence as an independent academic discipline, sociology should attempt to do at least three things. First, by definition, sociology is committed to showing the extent to which individual behaviour is a product of collective social life. Second, sociology must use theories, concepts and methods to provide accounts of social life which go beyond the understanding which we have as ordinary participating members of society. Third, it must demonstrate its theories and interpretations as objectively as possible; that is, it must do more than provide opinions and speculations.

In his study of suicide Durkheim tried to achieve these three objectives by demonstrating (1) that suicide rates were a product of society, (2) that the underlying causes of egoism, anomie and so on could only be understood by theoretical analysis, and (3) that these theories were in accord with the statistical 'facts' about suicide. The first two readings in this chapter illustrate Durkheim's approach. In Reading 5 Durkheim argues that the stability of the suicide rates is itself a *social fact* to be explained sociologically. The second extract (Reading 6) from *Suicide* examines Durkheim's discussion of egoistic suicide. As we observed in Chapter 3, Durkheim's approach provided a framework within which other sociologists have developed theories of suicide. Reading 7, taken from Henry and Short's ingenious 'modification' of Durkheim's theory, explains the concept of external restraint.

Most criticism of Durkheim's approach to suicide has come

from two sources. First, there are those outside sociology who feel that Durkheim understated the role of 'individual' influences in general and mental illness in particular in the causation of suicide. Second, some sociologists hold a very different view of the nature of the sociological task from that advanced by Durkheim. Reading 8, from Giddens's discussion of 'The Suicide Problem in French Sociology', illustrates the first line of criticism, while Reading 9, from Douglas's work, is an example of the second, sociological criticism.

Reading 5   The suicide rate as a social fact

Durkheim asks first why suicide should be of interest to the sociologist. He then goes on to outline the nature of the socio-logical task.

If, instead of seeing in [suicides] only separate occurrences, unrelated and to be separately studied, the suicides committed in a given society during a given period of time are taken as a whole, it appears that this total is not simply a sum of inde-pendent units, a collective total, but is itself a new fact *sui generis*, with its own unity, individuality and consequently its own nature – a nature, furthermore, dominantly social. . . . Accordingly, to a much higher degree than the death-rate, it is peculiar to each social group where it can be considered as a characteristic index. It is even so closely related to what is

Table III – Rate of suicides per million inhabitants in the different European countries

	Period			Numerical Position in the		
	1866–70	1871–73	1874–78	1 period	2 period	3 period
Italy	30	35	38	1	1	1
Belgium	66	69	78	2	3	4
England	67	66	69	3	2	2
Norway	76	73	71	4	4	3
Austria	78	94	130	5	7	7
Sweden	85	81	91	6	5	5
Bavaria	90	91	100	7	6	6
France	135	150	160	8	9	9
Prussia	142	134	152	9	8	8
Denmark	277	258	255	10	10	10
Saxony	293	267	334	11	11	11

most deeply constitutional in each national temperament that the order in which the different societies appear in this respect remains almost exactly the same at very different periods. This is proved by examining this same table. During the three periods there compared, suicide has everywhere increased, but in this advance the various peoples have retained their respective distances from one another. Each has its own peculiar coefficient of acceleration.

The suicide-rate is therefore a factual order, unified and definite, as is shown by both its permanence and its variability. For this permanence would be inexplicable if it were not the result of a group of distinct characteristics, solidary one with another, and simultaneously effective in spite of different attendant circumstances; and this variability proves the concrete and individual quality of these same characteristics, since they vary with the individual character of society itself. In short, these statistical data express the suicial tendency with which each society is collectively afflicted.

(E. Durkheim, *Suicide*, Routledge & Kegan Paul, 1952, pp. 51–52)

Reading 6   On egoistic suicide

For Durkheim, the regularity of the suicide rates could only be explained sociologically; that is, in terms of different forms of social life. In order to see how Durkheim attempted this we shall look more closely at his discussion of egoistic suicide. Using the statistics, Durkheim showed that suicide rates varied according to religious conviction, marital status and family size and declined in periods of political crisis and war. From this he set up the following propositions:

1 Suicide varies inversely with the degree of integration of religious society.
2 Suicide varies inversely with the degree of integration of domestic society.
3 Suicide varies inversely with the degree of integration of political society.

This grouping shows that whereas these different societies have a moderating influence upon suicide, this is due not to special characteristics of each but to a characteristic common to all.

Religion does not owe its efficacy to the special nature of religious sentiments, since domestic and political societies both produce the same effects when strongly integrated. This, moreover, we have already proved when studying directly the manner of action of different religions upon suicide. Inversely, it is not the specific nature of the domestic or political tie which can explain the immunity they confer, since religious society has the same advantage. The cause can only be found in a single quality possessed by all these social groups, though perhaps to varying degrees. The only quality satisfying this condition is that they are all strongly integrated social groups. So we reach the general conclusion: suicide varies inversely with the degree of integration of the social groups of which the individual forms a part.

(E. Durkheim, *Suicide*, Routledge & Kegan Paul, 1952, pp. 208–9)

It is important to grasp that Durkheim was *not* arguing that religion, the family and the political climate were separate factors causing suicide. Rather, he was arguing that they were all *visible* indicators of a hidden underlying cause, the degree of social integration.

Reading 7   External restraint

While some sociological studies of suicide rates merely test aspects of Durkheim's theory against new data, others attempt to 'modify', or 'clarify', the theory itself. In answering the question of why individuals enmeshed in social relationships are less inclined towards suicide, Henry and Short propose the notion of external restraint.

[The] behaviour of a person involved in a 'social' relationship as defined will be subject to a greater degree of 'horizontal external restraint' than behaviour of a person not involved in a social relationship. Further, as the number of social relationships in which the person is involved increases, the amount of horizontal external restraint over his behaviour will increase. The degree to which the person's behaviour is required to conform with the demands and expectations of others increases with the number of social relationships in which the person is involved. We have shown that the risk of suicide decreases as the number of social relationships increases. Since the degree of horizontal external restraint over behaviour increases with the number of relationships, let us suggest tentatively that the risk of suicide decreases as the degree to which behaviour is required to conform to the demands and expectations of others increases. Behaviour of the isolated person is freed from the requirement that it conform to the expectations of others. And the risk of suicide for the isolated is very high. . . .

Why does external restraint over behaviour provide this immunity? As the degree to which behaviour is determined and controlled by the demands and expectations of others increases, the share of others in responsibility for the consequences of the behaviour also increases. If a person commits an act primarily because others want him to commit it, others must share in the responsibility for the consequences of the act. The restraining persons can easily be blamed if the consequences of the act are unfortunate. But when an act is determined exclusively by the self and is independent of the wishes and expectations of others, the self must bear sole responsibility if it results in frustration. Others cannot be blamed since others were not involved in the determination of the act.

(A. Henry and J. Short, 'The Sociology of Suicide' in E. Shneidman and N. Farberow (eds), *Clues to Suicide*, New York, McGraw-Hill, 1957, pp. 64–5)

Reading 8   The debate on suicide and society

Suicide was not translated into English until 1952, but Giddens has documented the response to the book in French academic life. In general, while it was supported by the sociologically inclined, it was often attacked by those committed to a psychological or a 'disease' model of human behaviour.

The publication of *Le Suicide* stimulated divergent reactions in France. Durkheim's immediate disciples were prepared to adopt the text as a model of sociological method. Others, particularly in the field of psychology, were equally ready to reject entirely the claims for sociology advanced in the book. Most psychologists and psychiatrists continued to be heavily influenced by the 'psychiatric thesis', stemming from the position established by Esquirol, in relation to suicide. This thesis entailed the following four propositions: (1) suicide is always the product of some psychopathological condition; (2) the causes of suicide must thus be sought in the causes of the relevant types of mental disorder; (3) these causes are biological rather than social; (4) sociology can therefore make little if any contribution to the analysis of suicide.

The foundations were thus laid for a controversy which, although part of a broader conflict between Durkheim's advocacy of sociology as an autonomous discipline and the resistance of its detractors, did not become fully-developed until the period following the First World War, after the death of Durkheim himself.

The first major assault on Durkheim's position was launched in 1924 by de Fleury, a psychiatrist, in his *L'Angoisse humaine*. Following broadly the theoretical standpoint established by Esquirol, and supporting his argument with case-history material, de Fleury reiterated that suicide is always derivative of mental disorder, the causes of which are biopsychological rather than social. Suicidal tendencies, he concluded, are found mainly in persons suffering from cyclical depressive disorder (cyclothymia). This type of affective disorder, stated de Fleury, depends upon inherited characteristics of temperament: the disposition to suicide is biologically 'built into' such individuals. The tendency to states of morbid depression, moreover, according to de Fleury, develops largely independently of the objective circumstances of the individual. It is of little consequence, therefore, whether the individual is integrated into a group or not. While fluctuations in suicide rates can possibly be linked in a very crude way to social or economic changes, their role in the aetiology of suicide is even then only a secondary one: such changes may only serve to partially 'cluster' the suicides of individuals who would in any case kill themselves at a later date. The state of morbid anxiety into which depressive individuals periodically lapse, wrote de Fleury, 'is, in the immense majority of cases, the only cause of suicide'.

(A. Giddens, 'The Suicide Problem in French Sociology', in A. Giddens (ed.), *The Sociology of Suicide*, Cass, 1971, pp. 39–40)

Reading 9   'A new sociological method'

Not all criticism of the Durkheimian approach came from outside sociology. As we saw in Chapters 4 and 5, there was also criticism from those who favoured an interpretive view of sociology. In the next extract Douglas argues that, although Durkheim's theory *appears* to be supported by the evidence, this is not really the case. As Durkheim provided no clear operational definition of his key concepts (egoism and so on) he was able to 'read in' common-sense meanings that fitted his preconceived theory. Douglas goes on to call for a 'new' sociological approach, geared towards understanding the variety of meanings that suicide has in specific social contexts.

> Though the details are very difficult, the general nature of the remedy is clear: in order to determine and analyse the social meanings of suicide, and thence, to be able to determine what causal relations exist between these meanings and the various types of suicidal actions, sociologists must develop scientific methods of observing, describing and analysing communicative actions concerning real-world cases of suicide. Since we have already seen the fundamental weaknesses of the early case study method, this earlier method will not help much. The twentieth century case study methods of psychiatry and psychology are also of little use, since they are based primarily on certain abstract, predetermined, genetic theories of action which leave out of consideration almost all aspects of social meanings and, thereby, falsify the nature of human action.
>
> What is called for is a whole new sociological method for determining and analysing the communicative actions which can be observed and replicated in real-world cases of suicide. This method must retain the emphasis on observation and description of the earlier case-study methods, but it must also retain the emphasis on comparative studies of patterns of meanings of the statistical method.
>
> (J. Douglas, 'The Sociological Analysis of the Social Meanings of Suicide', *European Journal of Sociology* 1966, pp. 252–53)

Questions

1 In order to justify itself as an independent academic discipline, what objectives did Durkheim see sociology as having to attain?
2 How did Durkheim explain the relationship between suicide and religion, family and political crisis?
3 What is external restraint and how might it be related to suicide?
4 Outline the basis of the main critical responses to the Durkheimian approach to suicide.

9 Suicide and self-injury: case-study and documentary analysis

Introduction

Chapter 6 raised the question of what we mean by a suicidal act and how we might begin to classify and explain not just completed, or fatal, suicide, but a complex variety of suicidal behaviours. Readings 10 and 11, by **Firth** and **Stengel**, both stress the importance of examining not only the suicidal act itself but also the social response to it. They draw us towards taking a wider view of suicide and challenge conventional use of the term.

Sociologists who do not study suicide rates tend to use more ethnographic sources of data – for example, case histories, documentary data such as notes, diaries or autobiographies, and interviews with the 'survivors' of suicidal acts. **Stephens** based her research on interviews with 'suicidal women', and her conclusions are summarised in Reading 12. Although much work in this area of suicide research is directed towards explaining the suicidal actions of particular social groups, such as ethnic minorities, adolescents and particular occupational groups, there have been some attempts to construct general theories of suicidal action which provide a 'full' sociological alternative to the traditional sociological studies of suicide rates. **Baechler**'s study of suicide, from which Reading 13 is taken, adopts a 'Weberian' interpretive approach. In contrast, my own study of suicidal meanings, outlined in Reading 14, owes much more to Durkheim in inspiration, even though it examines case studies and not suicide rates.

Reading 10   Suicide in Tikopia

In his anthropological study of Tikopia, a Polynesian community in the western Pacific, Firth noticed that one 'suicidal' response to a critical situation was for the distressed individual either to swim or canoe out in the dangerous shark-infested waters. Here he describes the social response to such an act, and draws some sociological conclusions.

> As soon as news of a suicide swim or voyage is known, a searching fleet of canoes is organized and hastily paddles out in chase of the fugitive. If the attempt is really serious, the fleet's chances of success are not very high – the escapee goes off at night, or in a high wind, which militates against the likelihood of his being spotted and caught in those huge ocean wastes. But if the potential suicide rushes off in a rage at once, when sea conditions are good, or if his or her absence is noticed at once, or if the searching fleet is lucky or guesses well the effects of wind and current, the person may be recovered. For many of these attempts, especially by people who set off in daylight or in good conditions of wind and sea, it is very difficult indeed to decide just what combination of motives and chances lay behind their calculations – or whether they made any conscious calculations at all. . . . .
>
> Sociologically, two points of importance emerge from all this. The first is that the returned 'suicide' voyager by these procedures is completely reintegrated with society. His effort at detachment has failed, but he has succeeded in resolving his problem. He is once again absorbed and an effective catharsis has been obtained. The second point is that since a returned adventurer becomes the centre of attention, a certain premium is attached to attempting a dramatic sea flight of this kind. The stakes are high: they involve a real gamble with death. But if a man can go out, stay away for a while, and then return, he has a windfall gain in immediate social status. Yet cases of return from a distance would appear to be very rare; usually if a man is not found in the course of the day, he is lost to Tikopia – although in rare instances he may fetch up on another island.
>
> (R. Firth, 'Suicide and Risk-taking in Tikopia Society', *Psychiatry* 24, 1961, pp. 1–17)

Reading 11   Suicidal behaviour

In this extract Stengel suggests how an 'outside observer' would report on suicidal behaviour in modern society. He compares this imaginary account with the conventional notion of a suicidal act.

If a visiting scholar from one of the inhabited planets came to earth to study the human species, he would sooner or later notice that some humans sometimes commit acts of self-injury. He would observe that occasionally this self-damaging behaviour causes the person's death, but it would hardly occur to him that this relatively rare outcome is the main purpose of that behaviour. Having been taught that careful observation of as many subjects as possible is essential before one draws conclusions about the purpose of a certain type of behaviour, and having also learned that the subjects' explanations can be highly misleading, he would watch as many such acts as possible, together with their antecedents and consequences, without preconceived ideas, over a fairly long period. His report on his observations would read like this: 'There are some humans who damage themselves more or less badly and in about one in eight cases the damage is so severe that they die. Whatever the outcome, most of them give a hint or a clear warning to one or several of their fellow humans well before the act, telling them that they are thinking of killing themselves. Those fellow humans may or may not take notice of this warning. But once a person is found to have committed an act of self-damage there is invariably a great commotion among the other humans. They clearly show that they wish the act had never been committed. They do everything to keep him alive and to undo the damage that he did to himself. They go even further than this. While they usually do not show much concern about and sympathy with the suffering of fellow humans, an act of self-injury by one of themselves seems to make them take a profound and most active interest in him, at least for a time. They behave as if they had to help him and to put him on his feet. As a result, his situation is transiently or permanently transformed for the better. These helpful reactions are particularly marked in the members of his family group, but the larger community to which the human belongs also takes part.

'If one looked at the acts of self-damage alone one would be led to believe that self-destruction is their only purpose. But if one considers certain antecedents and the consequences of these acts, this simple explanation cannot be sustained. Why should these humans so often warn others of their intention to damage themselves, especially as they must know that this kind of behaviour is dreaded in their family group and the community? They must also know that, once they have injured themselves, everybody will be upset and will want to help them, and if they should die, many other humans will feel they ought to have helped them. It looks as if their peculiar behaviour cannot be derived from one single tendency but is probably due to a combination of at least two tendencies, one of which might be the urge to self-damage and possibly self-destruction, the other the urge to make other humans show concern and love and act accordingly. There are other peculiar features in the self-damaging behaviour of humans, but these seem the most important.'

The purpose of this fictitious report from unprejudiced space is to bring home the need for a new and very careful look at suicidal behaviour. The most striking difference between the conventional view of suicidal acts and that of the unprejudiced observer lies in his emphasis on the reactions of the environment. The possibility of such reactions and their occasional exploitation has long been known, but this is believed to occur only in suicidal attempts regarded as non-genuine. All genuine suicidal acts are understood to aim at death alone. It is this notion which the uncommitted observer refuses to accept.

(E. Stengel, *Suicide and Attempted Suicide*, Penguin, 1973)

Although Firth is writing about a supposedly 'primitive' society and Stengel is observing suicidal behaviour in modern society, it is interesting to note the similarities in both accounts. In this context it is also instructive to observe that, while suicidal actions 'for others' or for a 'higher ideal' are seen by many as being confined to 'primitive' societies, examples of such 'sacrificial suicides' can be found in modern societies.

R. Léopold. He worked all his life in the vineyard. He raised three children. At 65 he lost his wife and sensed the decline of his strength. His children asked him to 'make his bestowals,' that is, to distribute his goods in exchange for life annuity or a food allowance. He divided his goods into two parts, one for his son, the other for his daughter, and said they were to make a settlement with a brother who worked abroad. The brother and sister agreed to feed 'the old man,' taking turns a week at a time, with shellfish, bread, potatoes, and two or three litres of wine a day. After several years his children began to find he was costing them a good deal, and told him so. One day in August, his daughter found him hanged in the coach house that served as a wine-storage room.

(J. Baechler, *Suicides*, Blackwell, 1979)

A woman had been chronically bedridden for 20 years. . . . Gradually the husband began to express his distaste for his own care-giving role, to blame his wife more and more for the constriction imposed on his own activities, and to voice barely disguised antipathy toward her for continuing to live. He verbally projected the picture of what he would be 'robbed of' in the future, but at the same time expressed concern for her very real physical pain and continued his nursing activities. As the neighbourhood deteriorated over the years, he began to talk of burglaries and purchased a gun which he discharged in a 'how to work it' session; he then left the loaded gun within arm's reach of his bed-ridden wife. After the demonstration and a particularly bitter soliloquy, the husband went to work. The wife killed herself shortly afterwards.

(S. Taylor, *Durkheim and the Study of Suicide*, Macmillan, 1982)

Reading 12   Women and self-harm

Interviews with those who survive suicidal acts provide researchers with an important source of data. **Stephens**, in interviews with 50 women attempters of suicide, focused on their relationships with men. She found four recurring themes in the interviews: (1) over-dependence on the male partner; (2) infidelity; (3) brutality and battery; and (4) denial of affection. Like other researchers in this area, Stephens emphasises that many suicidal acts have to be understood as the product of a *relationship* rather than traits 'within' the suicidal individual alone. In the following extract she summarises the implications of her research.

What emerges from the present study is a description of the specific conflicts that suicidal women experience in some of their most important and intimate relationships; i.e. with their men. It is undeniable that these are unhappy, even pathological relationships in which the women have experienced a lack of love, have been beaten and brutalized, have suffered sexual betrayal and have developed deep feelings of worthlessness and despair. . . .

The commonality which all of these women share are their feelings of low self-esteem, powerlessness, and worthlessness – self-negating feelings that have been exacerbated in their relationships with their partners. From their point of view, their partners are veritable 'villains'; however as we have noted, this study looked only at the perceptions and experiences of the suicidal women. Clearly, the men's experiences constitute an area in which research is needed in order to understand fully the interpersonal context of the suicide process.

Finally, we do not mean to suggest that other relationships are not also important in the genesis of suicide attempting. Although beyond the scope of the present paper, research into other significant relationships of suicidal women will complete the emerging framework of interpersonal conflict that appears to characterize suicidal women. We know that female suicidal careers are intensely interpersonal processes whose full explanation will elude us until we also understand the accompanying careers of all the significant others whose role in the genesis of suicidal acts is so powerful.

(B. Stephens, 'Suicidal Women and Their Relationships with Husbands, Boyfriends and Lovers', *Suicide and Life Threatening Behaviour*, Vol. 15, 1985, pp. 88–89)

My own research into female overdosing tends to confirm these observations. The high rates of overdosing in women, particularly young women, tend to be related to their position in society. . . .

Modern women, particularly younger women, are placed in a position where, on the one hand society encourages them to believe that they are in every respect the equal of men and should think of themselves as such while, on the other hand, systematically denying them the opportunity to compete on equal terms.

Increasing numbers of women are, therefore, vulnerable to what social scientists call anomie, a disproportion between expectation and achievement, the resulting frustrations of which make, among other things, the resort to self poisoning more likely.

(S. Taylor, 'Why Should an Overdose Seem the Best Medicine?, *Guardian*, 27 April 1983)

Reading 13   Suicidal meanings

In *Suicides*, Baechler, following the approach advocated by Douglas, begins by examining case studies of individual suicides. He identifies eleven distinct suicidal meanings which he groups into four types. The following extract illustrates Baechler's general approach and his attempt to classify recurring patterns of meanings of suicidal acts into a typology.

Now the present problem concerns the meaning of suicide, and the proposed method to study it is that of Weber's ideal types. Practically speaking, this amounts to an analysis of as many cases as possible in order to determine if one can distinguish and isolate (by a one-side exaggeration of certain traits) one or several meanings. Or to be more precise, and to make use of what was established in Part One, can one distinguish several typically distinct situations where suicidal action could be considered as an adequate solution? I will now list the ideal types that I have been able to construct before devoting the rest of Part Two to the detailed analysis of them. I distinguish eleven types of suicide that may usefully be grouped together in four more general types.

The first general type is indicated by the adjective *escapist* and designates all cases of suicide where the general meaning or sense of the act is to take flight, where in consequence suicide appears as a means of escaping something. One can distinguish three suicidal *subtypes*:

1 *Flight*: an escape from a situation sensed by the subject to be intolerable.
2 *Grief*: occurs following the loss of a central element of the subject's personality or way of life.
3 *Punishment*: occurs in order to expiate a real or imaginary fault.

The second general type is *aggressive* because the end sought is, in fact, an act of aggression perpetrated against another. By killing oneself or by trying to do so, the subject seeks to harm somebody else. There are four *subtypes*:

1 *Vengeance*: is intended either to provoke another's remorse or to inflict the opprobrium of the community on him.
2 *Crime*: involves another in one's own death.

3 *Blackmail*: puts pressure on another by depriving him of something he holds dear.

4 *Appeal*: informs one's friends and neighbours that the subject is in danger (the suicidal act is a sort of alarm signal).

Death takes on yet a third radically distinct meaning in what I call the *oblative* type. Here there are two *subtypes*:

1 *Sacrifice*: seeks to save or to gain a value judged to be greater than personal life.

2 *Transfiguration*: seeks to attain a state considered by the subject to be infinitely more delightful.

Finally, self-destruction can take its meaning as what one may call a *ludic* type. It has two subtypes.

1 *Ordeal*: entails risking one's life in order to prove oneself to oneself or to solicit the judgment of others.

2 *Game*: is to take a chance on killing oneself where the sole purpose is to play with one's own life.

(J. Baechler, *Suicides*, Blackwell, 1979)

Reading 14   *Risk taking and purposive suicide*

In contrast to the 'Weberian' approach employed by Baechler, I argued in an earlier work that interpretation of the meaning of suicidal actions comes not from immersion in the 'lived-in' world of the actor, but through the general meanings derived from theoretical analysis. The following extract explores the relationship between risk-taking, ordeal suicide and more determined and purposeful attempts to end life.

Ordeals are suicidal acts of uncertainty, where the individual is seeking to validate the meaning of his or her existence. This is illustrated in the following cases:

A 40-year-old male schizophrenic left home in a state of depression. He was brought home by the police; though watched, he slipped away and locked himself in the lavatory. He opened the door only after his wife had implored him to do so. He had a towel round his neck soaked in blood; there were two long cuts under the skin. He declared that he had made the suicide attempt 'as an act of faith, to prove whether God wanted him to live or die'.

The poet, Sylvia Plath, for much of the later part of her life experienced the feeling of being stalked by death. She survived one serious suicide attempt in her youth, and years later, confessed to a friend that a recent car 'accident' she had survived had been quite deliberate. She had driven off the road knowing full well that it *might* kill her. However, having survived, she was then able to write freely about the act because it was behind her. The car crash, like the previous suicidal attempt, became 'another death' that she had 'come through'. She felt that death was something that had to be confronted periodically.

Devoted churchgoer Denys Christian believed that God would save him in a leap from his thirteenth floor flat. . . . So despite warnings from his wife he went ahead with the ultimate test . . . and died. [His wife] told an inquest at Southwark, London, yesterday that her 26-year-old husband stepped on to a balcony and balanced on a six inch ledge. . . . She said: 'Four days before his death he said he would jump to prove his faith in God. He told me nothing would happen to him'. . . . A parishioner friend said 'We never thought he would go to these lengths to prove his faith.'. . .

Suicidal actions of this nature may be directly contrasted in one respect with those where individuals resort to suicide from a psychological sense of complete certainty. Such might be the case, for example, for the depressive who now 'knows' that his life is one long, dark tunnel with *no* hope of light at the end, or for one who is chronically sick and realises that he has but a few painful months in which to linger on. For some, there may seem little point in pressing on into a future that is already 'known' and is beyond all doubt. Those in such situations may develop a desire to die arising from a fatalistic acceptance that, to all intents and purposes, life is already over. I have referred to this as *submissive suicide*. Whereas the [ordeal suicide] has become uncertain about the rules of the game and its results, the submissive suicide recognises that for him the game is irretrievably over and lost. He therefore knows everything worth knowing because, having established that for him life is over, knowledge that may once have been important (such as the state of his bank balance) is now irrelevant. In submissive suicide the act will therefore be 'serious', or purposive, as opposed to ludenic, and thus more *likely* to be fatal, for the individual is not confronting death in an ordeal to resolve the uncertainty of whether he is dead or alive, but is embracing death because to all intents and purposes he is already dead. Death is not seen as a 'competitor', or a 'judge' as in [the ordeal], but more of an ally, a friend helping the defeated individual leave the field with a little dignity and grace. While in the ordeal the individual is asking *Who am I?*, the submissive suicide is saying *I am dead*. In performances of submissive suicide, we find the individual expressing defeat, resignation, loss of hope. For example:

A 62-year-old woman dying of lymphosarcoma. During the three weeks prior to her suicide she had repeatedly said, 'I'm through. I'm whipped. This is the end. I can't take it any longer.' During the final week she added, 'I will not die a lingering death'. On the morning of her suicide, she kissed her husband goodbye as he was leaving for work and said to him, 'Darling, this is your last kiss'. She committed suicide later that morning.

Jean Gray, after a somewhat unsatisfactory life with several successive husbands, found herself at the age of thirty-three deserted by her husband, estranged from her parents, and with an adolescent daughter. Cancer developed, and when Mrs Gray could no longer work, her daughter found work which supported them, since relatives refused to assist. . . . When the cancer became serious, she committed suicide, leaving the following letters. 'To My Daughter Alice: Baby please forgive me for not trying to struggle along any longer but I am at the end. It is of no use to try. Please try to live up to my teaching and be a pure sweet girl always and if you love Arthur and he is still willing to marry you, why you have my consent, although I realise that you are very young, but if you had someone to protect you and provide for you it would be a whole lot better for you, as, my dear, you will find this world a pretty hard place to live in, but be brave and make the best of things. I wish I could stay with you a while longer but it cannot be done. With love, Your Mother.' To her doctors she wrote: 'I know you have done all you could to try to save me but I realise it cannot be done. I thank you for all you have done and I know there is no use to try to struggle any longer.'

It is into this context that we can place the activities and demands of those who seek changes in public attitudes and the law regarding voluntary euthanasia. . . .
(S. Taylor, *Durkheim and the Study of Suicide*, Macmillan, 1982, pp. 167–69)

Questions

1 What are the most important similarities in the accounts of suicidal behaviour given by Firth and Stengel?
2 Why does Stengel argue that there is 'a need for a new and careful look at suicidal behaviour'?
3 What are the main conclusions that Stephens draws from her study of suicidal women?
4 Why might the high incidence of self-poisoning in younger women be related to their role in society?
5 Outline Baechler's approach to the study of the meanings of suicidal behaviour and compare it to that advocated by Durkheim.
6 How does Taylor explain the difference between ordeal and purposive suicidal acts?

10   Summary and conclusions

The purpose of this brief chapter is to outline some of the main issues in the sociology of suicide.

1 The study of suicide has become a very important topic for sociology. The attempt to show that such an apparently isolated, detached and seemingly 'anti-social' act as suicide is in fact influenced by society provides sociology with one of its greatest challenges.

2 Following Durkheim, most sociologists have made a distinction between the explanation of the suicide rate and the explanation of individual cases of suicide. Sociology has tended to see its primary task as explaining differences in suicide rates. It has been argued that the consistency of differences in suicide rates is caused by social influences.

3 Among the most important causes identified by sociologists have been individuals' lack of social ties, changes in social status, social disorganisation, deviance and socialisation practices which result in individuals directing feelings of failure inwards at themselves.

4 One of the main lines of criticism of this approach has come from research into the 'social construction' of official suicide statistics. Some of this research has suggested that official suicide rates are an unsuitable source of data for 'traditional' research purposes. In this context, it is important to distinguish between problems of reliability and problems of validity of official statistics.

5 Interpretive studies provide the main sociological alternative to the traditional sociological approach to suicide. This approach – which makes a fundamental distinction between the study of the natural world and the study of the social world – advocates the importance of beginning research by trying to 'understand' the 'situated meanings' of individual cases of suicide, then identifying more general patterns of meanings.

6 Another important criticism of traditional (sociological and non-sociological) approaches to suicide comes from those who

question the conventional notion of the suicidal act. Detailed research into the micro-social contexts of suicidal acts has shown that the majority of them, rather being aimed at death alone, are undertaken with confused or ambivalent intentions.

7 Recently, sociologists have moved away from an exclusive concern with fatal, or completed, suicide and have begun exploring non-fatal suicidal actions, the relationship between risk taking and 'purposive' suicidal actions and have begun to construct more general theories of suicidal behaviour.

Questions

1 To what extent was Durkheim successful in explaining suicide sociologically?
2 Compare and contrast the 'traditional' and 'interpretive' sociological approaches to suicide.
3 What are the main arguments against the use of official suicide statistics in sociological research into suicide?
4 'Most suicidal acts are Janus-faced, orientated towards death and dying and life and survival.' (Stengel) What are the implications of this observation for sociological research into suicide and self-injury?

Projects and exercises

1 *Theoretical approaches to suicide.* Two or three members of a group argue the case for a 'Durkheimian' approach to suicide as favourably as they can. Two or three others then criticise the 'traditional', or 'Durkheimian', approach and put the case for the 'interpretive' approach advocated by Douglas and others. Other members of the group then say which approach, or which aspects of each approach, they find most convincing and why. Is it possible to combine, or synthesise, the two approaches? Are there some studies of suicidal behaviour by sociologists that fit into neither the 'Durkheimian' or 'interpretive' frameworks?
2 *'Lay' and 'expert' explanations of suicide.* Members of the sociology group should collect as many newspaper accounts of suicidal behaviour as they can. Most of these accounts will contain an 'explanation' for the suicide, for instance, 'lonely widower kills himself' and so on. Write down the 'lay'

explanations that you discover and compare them to academic, or 'expert' explanations (such as egoism or status change). What are the main differences and similarities between the 'lay' and 'expert' theories? Where there is overlap, how are we to account for it, and what are the implications for sociological explanation? (For further guidance on this issue, see J. Atkinson, *Discovering Suicide*, chap. 7.)

3 *Coroner's inquiry*. Three people in a group are selected as the coroner and his or her officials. A case is referred to them where a few facts from the circumstances of death are known; for example, a body found in the local canal. It is the officials' job to decide whether or not the person committed suicide or not. The officials then write down what they want to know about the biography of the deceased – such as his or her age, or whether he or she was married or unmarried. The answers to these preliminary questions can be provided either by the class teacher or by randomly selected 'answer cards'. On the basis of the information they receive, the officials then decide whom they wish to interview at the inquest (see Chapter 4), and other members of the class are selected to play the relevant parties (including family doctor, spouse or teacher). Once the inquest is completed, the coroner's team have to decide whether the death was suicide, accident, or whether to give an open verdict, and they must explain to the court *why* they came to that decision. If *particular* answers had been different would they have come to a different decision? What does this exercise tell us about how coroners come to decisions in the ' real' world? (For further guidance on this issue, see S. Taylor, *Durkheim and the Study of Suicide*, chaps. 4–5.)

Further reading

General sociological texts

A. Bilton *et al.*, *Introductory Sociology*, Macmillan, 1981.
Contains a section on suicide (pp. 608–25), which considers some of the main issues. However, the interpretation of Durkheim is generally weak and simply wrong in places, while the interpretive alternative is advanced without any critical analysis.

E. Cuff *et al.*, *Perspectives in Sociology*, Allen and Unwin, 1984.
Uses the example of suicide to illustrate sociological perspectives and research strategies but, again, presents a very weak account of Durkheim's work and uses a very limited range of sources on suicidal behaviour.

On Durkheim

K. Thompson, *Durkheim*, Tavistock, 1982.
An excellent, clear, well-written and straightforward text on Durkheim, including a chapter on suicide. The best book of its kind on Durkheim.

On suicide rates

J. Atkinson, *Discovering Suicide*, Macmillan, 1978.
Documents Atkinson's work on coroners and the progression and development of his ideas on social theory.

Sociology of suicide

J. Douglas, *The Social Meanings of Suicide*, Princeton University Press, 1967.

An interesting, though complex, book going into difficult philosophical ideas in some detail. A book to 'dip into' rather than read from cover to cover.

A. Giddens (ed.), *The Sociology of Suicide*, Cass, 1971.

The only general 'reader' on the sociology of suicide; contains some classic material from Firth, Stengel, Douglas and others but is now rather dated.

S. Taylor, *Durkheim and the Study of Suicide*, Macmillan, 1982.

Contains a general overview of the sociology of suicide from Durkheim onwards, original research into suicide statistics and the context of suicidal actions.

Index